**PRAISE FOR**

MW00883664

"Angeline has cr... ...que way to look at men. Her Man-imals will surely become buzz-words in the relationship arena! Deep insights and psychological principles are presented in fresh and interesting ways as she writes with a heart of compassion for the struggles of single women."

— Lisa Sasevich, The Queen of Sales Conversion

"Angeline's book has provided me with a blueprint for successfully partnering with another. The communication and boundary skills I learned (or more accurately, didn't learn) early in life have not served me well. What I have learned from Angeline has already impacted my relationships - and it's not been limited to romantic relationships, it's relevant for all relationships. I've been fortunate to work directly with Angeline, she is kind, compassionate and very insightful. The first time I spoke with her I was bitter, jaded and very resistant. By the end of the 1-hour phone call, which morphed into 2 hours, I felt hopeful. That was something I haven't felt in a very long time. You'll learn much from reading (and rereading) her book. If what she has to say really resonates with you I encourage you to reach out to her. You won't be sorry!"

— Shelly Ross, San Francisco, CA

*"Angeline has done a masterful job of combining the best nuggets of wisdom from some of the best books on relationships! Better yet, she does so clearly and succinctly so you can learn all the principles you need to improve your relationships by actually getting to the end of the book! I am grateful for the heightened awareness I gained of how I can improve my love life!"*

— Carol Andrews, Holistic Coach, Idaho

*"I LOVE the MAN-imal system. The way that Angeline identifies the different types of men and what motivates them is UNIQUE and infinitely helpful to any woman! This book is easily a new paradigm to support women to wisely date and choose a man that will be a satisfying partner for life!"*

— Elynn Light, Transformational Life Coach

*"I learned quite a bit and found compelling examples and stories. I especially recommend it as a gift from a beloved family member, teacher, or friend, to a mid-teens or older girl, who wants to read a different, and practical, view on relationships. I look forward to the book's potential being realized as it starts helping/healing relationships around the world."*

— David Manderscheid, Seattle, WA

*"A fabulous book, filled with tips to help you improve your relationships! I loved all the personal examples, especially the stories of Sarah interwoven throughout. They really helped me to relate the info to my own life!"*

— Katherine Cheney, Realtor, Utah

*"I have quite a few clients in my practice as a clinical psychologist who were at a loss how to choose a "good" guy, after themselves having had a very traumatic upbringing. I think this book can really be a sincere help in this matter. It is such a terrific struggle to change those old ingrained patterns. Angeline outlined the array of problematic and positive patterns very clearly, complete with a visual animal symbol to let it stick in our minds and hearts!!!! And then practicing how the "good" behavior looks, like learning to recognize a new car brand is a great analogy. I will definitely recommend it to my clients and friends."*

— Susan Dikken, Clinical Psychologist, Netherlands

*"Intelligent, important and life-changing is the best way to describe my experience reading this book. Unlike anything I have read before, Angeline uses common sense to approach dating relationships. Without a doubt, her wisdom will guide you out of the dating jungle and empower you to find your true-love relationship."*

— Michelle Schroeder, Product & Business Development

*"Angeline has created an empowering book that is entertaining to read. Her depth of relationship expertise, combined with a unique perspective, has allowed her to share her insight and experiences in truly meaningful ways. She relates analogies and stories that make the book's message easy to understand and apply. The principles contained in Gorillas Make Great Lovers! span multiple generations and are universally applicable in romantic and social relationships, as well one's relationship with the self. I recommend this book to all women who seek to increase their ability to effectively communicate and recognize their ideal man."*

— Joe Kaitschuck, Gray Man Consulting, Federal Way, WA

# Gorillas Make Great Lovers!

Escape the Dating Jungle,
Find an Ideal Man, and
Build a Life-long Love Affair.

By
Angeline M. Hart
with
Dixon A. Schwenk

Kindle Publishing Package

ISBN-13: 978-1533499653

ISBN-10: 1533499659

DISCLAIMER

Author's photo courtesy of Monique Feil

# Dedication

Dedicated to the memory of
Angeline's father,
Clifton D. Manderscheid,
the original Gorilla.

# Table of Contents

# Chapter 2: "I Can't Find Any Good Men!" 83

# Chapter 3: "Okay, I Admit, My Boundaries are a Hot Mess!" .................................. 101

## Chapter 4: "Why Do I Feel This Way?".. 133

## Chapter 5: "I Think I Have a Communication Problem!" ................... 153

## Chapter 6: "I Don't Think I Can Ever Trust a Man Again!" ........................................ 185

## Chapter 7: "What About Intimacy and Sex?" ..................................................... 205

She is balanced, tolerates no game-playing, and remains intent on you being authentic to you.

Through her methods, I have clarity that has transformed my old ways into new ones. I now understand how to live my life smarter and because of that, I have attracted much better men. Sure, I want to fall in love; but for the first time, I want to date and meet different men, be smart, and make sure they meet my qualifications before I commit. Most importantly, I want to know we can build something great. I can't express enough how powerful that stance is. Moreover, how it has given the keys to my life back.

Thank you Angeline, for writing this book, for believing in Love, and understanding where our hearts come from. Because of you, I have fallen into relationship with myself, which I never thought was possible. With your dedication to this work, I know I have the ability to pick a great guy and fall in love with the man of my dreams. But, this time around, I won't drag myself through the mud on the way there.

Our future partners will appreciate her work as well. I've received compliments from men on my communication, approach and clarity. I was recently told by a guy I have been dating, "I really appreciate how you approach us. It makes me feel good."

I am passionate about what works, and when Angeline asked me for my perspective on her book, I was eager to share my own experience. It excites me to think of others like me, readers following through these steps to learn basics in a fun, approachable way through this book—and hopefully receive coaching from Angeline herself. She is focused, smart and very committed to helping people finding their true-love relationship. Without a doubt, I can say she is a gift to us all!

Be brave. Her system works!

— *Michelle Schroeder*

February 16, 2016

# Preface

My mother, Lorraine Manderscheid, was a public school teacher for 17 years. Her caring and skill with her students was phenomenal, and many have grown to adulthood praising her for the difference she made in their lives. While teaching during the day, she also attended the local University at night to study psychology. Gradually, she got her Masters in Counseling, followed by a Doctorate in Educational Psychology.

Mom was the type of person who shared what she was experiencing in her life. She talked about what she was learning, and applied it wherever she saw a need. In my family, this meant our dinner conversations were frequently about psychological principles. For example, it was common for us to discuss the ways we were building or damaging trust within the family. In addition, Mom put all six of us kids through a year or more of psychotherapy.

Later, after opening her private practice, she was often asked to speak to women's groups. Her usual topics were family relations and communications. Mom often took one or more of us kids to share the stage with her, where she would have us role-play or demonstrate an interaction. As a young adult, I even attended workshops with her. Needless to say, I was immersed in psychology, and sometimes explained healthy relationship principles to my girlfriends when they shared emotional challenges with me.

I was allowed to start dating at age 16. Although only one boy from high school asked me out, by the time I was a junior in high school, I had discovered the boys at the local university. I dated a *lot* of them! I took a college boy to my junior prom and a different one to my senior prom. I went to college at Arizona State University, as they used to say, to earn my "MRS" degree. In other words, my goal was to get married and be a mom. A number of good guys talked to me about getting married, and I received three marriage proposals before I was married at age 22. I married a good man, the one my mother thought was right for me. We had three wonderful children. I was in love with being a wife and mother. I even loved being pregnant!

Unfortunately, although I "loved" my husband, I wasn't "in love" with him. We gradually grew apart, emotionally. We did not share our deep hearts with each other. Instead, when we differed, we treated each other with kindness and respect, but were not open and authentic. Rather than working through challenges, we compromised. We were co-dependent. Everything looked fine on the surface.

But, after 20 years, we divorced—amicably. Our friends were shocked and said, "How can you possibly divorce? You are our example of a good marriage!" I learned a lot about what does and doesn't work in relationships through the successes and failures of my first marriage, which I will share with you in this book.

I was a single mom for four years after divorcing my first husband, the father of my children. At the time we split, my children were ages 9, 14, and 15—and I was 42.

While I was single, I dated a lot. Again, men were talking with me about marriage. Then, at a dance, I met my Ideal Man, Dixon.

We were married just over a year later, and as of now, we've been together almost 25 years. He has become the perfect man for me! I'll share more about Dixon later.

The reason I share this part of my story with you is because, during all this time, from age 16 till the present, women have observed my consistent ability to discern and choose "good men." They often asked me, "Where do you find all of these good men?" I would guess you may be wondering, too.

One of my girlfriends, Betsy, who had been divorced, and subsequently dated a lot, once complained to me about the difficulty of finding a good man. I told her I would help her. So we went to a singles bar. I suggested Betsy look around, and point out a man she found attractive. She slowly scanned the dimly lit bar and then pointed out a man across the room. I'm not kidding when I say, I physically recoiled. I wasn't subtle with my feedback. I said, "From twenty feet away, I can see he's trouble!"

"Really? What do you see?" Betsy was more than curious.

I couldn't find the words to describe the negative aspects I saw in that man, compared to how a good man should look. I was surprised Betsy had overlooked these things, which were obvious to me. Up until that night, I thought any woman could see the difference.

So, I began a search for ways to describe good men, and how to help women recognize them. And women continued to ask me for help in finding good men.

As I looked for ways to describe different types of men, I gradually developed the 12 Man-imals profiles, which I will fully cover in Chapter 1. When I shared this unique concept with women, and helped them recognize an Ideal Man, they often asked me for additional help to apply this for themselves. They could see my happy marriage, the sweet fun between me and Dixon, and they wanted a relationship like ours. It was a natural transition for me to become a Relationship Coach, because I had already been "coaching" girls and women since I was 16.

Many people have encouraged me to write this book. They told me I offer a unique perspective as a coach. In this book, I will share my own experiences, along with those of my family, friends and clients (with their permission). Some of the names have been changed to give individuals privacy, of course.

In addition, I will share the psychological principles behind healthy relationships, many of which I learned from my own mother. It has become my passion and purpose to help women find love! It is the reason I am finally writing this book.

# Introduction

I'm hoping you bought this book because you want to find your Ideal Man and build a life-long Love Affair with him. I can help you do that! I'm going to share with you all the "secrets" I share with my coaching clients. This book holds the key to your dreams about love! But, just reading it won't make it happen. You will also need to do some work.

This book will help you figure out what has been getting in your way, and why your relationships aren't working. Together, we will assess your situation and become very clear about what you want in a man and in a relationship. I will share with you the skills you need to build and maintain a long-term loving relationship. You will also need to practice the skills I share with you. It will be a challenging and exciting journey. You CAN succeed at love! I know you can, because I have helped other women just like you. Are you ready? Let's go!

Most people learn best through stories. So I'm going to share lots of stories with you. Some of them are about me, my family and friends, and some are about my clients. In this book all the stories are true, but all the names (except my family members who agreed to be named) are false.

# Sarah's Story

When Sarah was five years old, she cut her sister's hair. This is actually a fairly common thing for young children to do. But her father over-reacted in a very damaging way. He told her she had been very bad and couldn't be in their family any more. He had her pack a small suitcase, and take her favorite doll. He then drove her to a distant neighborhood, and parked in front of a stranger's home. He told her to get out of the car, knock on their door, and ask if she could live with them. Of course she was upset, crying and begging to stay in the car, but he actually pushed her out and then drove away!

While still crying, Sarah walked up to the door with her little suitcase and doll. When she knocked on the door, a man opened it. She then asked if she could live with him, just as her father instructed. Of course this man was dumbfounded to find a small child crying on his doorstep, asking to live with him.

At this point, her father drove back and started yelling at Sarah to get back in the car. She did. And he told her, "See, he doesn't want you either. No one wants you." Then he drove her to a dirt crossroads in the country, where no houses could be seen. Again, he told her to get out of the car, and again he drove off—leaving her crying with her suitcase and doll. In tears, she sat down at the roadside.

A short while later, two young men in a pickup truck stopped and asked her if she needed help. Although she didn't know it, her father was parked where he could see her. At this point he drove back, and yelled at her to get in the car. She did, and he told her again, "No one wants you and I don't either, but I guess you'll have to stay with us for now." He then took her home.

Perhaps you can imagine the devastation this deeply abusive behavior caused in this young child. We depend on our parents to care for and protect us, we really are helpless and fragile when we are very young. We naturally trust, even when it isn't deserved. When a parent severely betrays that trust, it is deeply damaging to the psyche of a child and the negative effects are long term, even after the betrayal itself may be forgotten. These betrayals are often not singular events, either, and the pattern and repetition further reinforces a child's emotional injury. This incident is only one of many ways this man damaged his daughter's belief in her value.

At the age of 40, Sarah became my client. Although she is an unusually beautiful woman, she has never had a long-term, stable relationship. She has had many short-term relationships, the longest of which lasted only two years. Most of them ended in some form of betrayal or abandonment. Men who acted like her father!

Why did she choose men who abandoned her like her father did? You might think she would try to avoid that. And she did try to avoid it! But here's the thing, we carry the dysfunctional patterns we learned in childhood, and we subconsciously act accordingly, even when we are consciously trying to avoid the things that have caused us pain.

But, we CAN break the negative relationship patterns we carry! Within just five weeks of coaching, this lovely young woman is making great progress. Initially, we used The Gorilla Quiz to identify what she wants in an Ideal Man. She is learning to recognize the difference between her Ideal Man and the losers she previously dated. She is finding better candidates for repeat dates. She is learning to know the difference between men who behave badly (like her father) and men who are more emotionally healthy. She also is learning to set and maintain boundaries to protect herself from emotional abuse. For the first time in her life, Sarah feels empowered. And even more importantly, she realizes she has value and is worth the effort to choose only good men to invite into her life.

Four months from when she started coaching, Sarah may have found the man of her dreams. She actually met him previously through a dating website, and even went on a first date. But, back then, she didn't have the awareness to recognize what she really wants. Back then, she was still looking for "flashy" men, which was what society told her was desirable, but wasn't what her heart actually needed. After some coaching, and using The Gorilla Quiz to identify her preferences, she gave this man another chance, and now thinks she may have found her Ideal Man. He is intellectually oriented, seems emotionally mature, and she looks forward to getting to know him better.

Sarah is learning that building love is really a process, like building a house.

In this book I'm going to share a lot of Sarah's story, but Sarah is not unique. Many women can relate to some part of her dating and personal history, as she worked this program faithfully, while being very honest with herself and open to change.

You can learn the same "secrets" that Sarah is learning. You can find your Ideal Man and build a long-term Love Affair with him! This book, and some additional resources at my website, will provide a map to guide you on this quest.

# Chapter 1:

# Your Ideal Man and the 12 Man-imals

*"Of course I am not worried about intimidating men. The type of man who will be intimidated by me is exactly the type of man I have no interest in."*

— Chimamanda Ngozi Adichie

# How Do You Find Your Ideal Man?

Today, society and the media (celebrity magazines, movies, romance novels...never mind the commercials) will try to sell you on a certain idea for your Ideal Man. He looks like Magic Mike, dresses like GQ, and drives a flashy new (and always clean) car. And if you have any doubts, the sexual chemistry is off the charts! Well, I'm here to tell you, they are wrong!

Do you remember the story about Sarah? Her father was an extremely poor parent. The example he offered Sarah in the ways of men made it difficult for Sarah to recognize good men. Many women are faced with this challenge.

## A Good Man

When it comes to recognizing good men, I have an unfair advantage, because I had an excellent father. Clifton Manderscheid was an Oklahoma farm boy who loved the land and was kind to animals. He was physically strong from working in the fields, and from being the "key" man on his small town, high school's varsity sports teams. He was the youngest son in a family of seven children, having five brothers and one sister. Clif was valedictorian of his class and was offered a college football scholarship. He turned it down, because he wanted to go to a different college, which provided a better agronomy program. He was the first in his family to attend college. Although he didn't marry until he was 32, he and my Mom, Lorraine, had 7 children (of which I am the eldest).

My father was devoted to his family. He was easy-going and fair, and avoided physical discipline. Although he was intensely masculine, he was also a gentleman. I don't remember ever hearing him yell, and the first time I heard him swear, I was 18 and I was actually the reason he said "Hell." My dad was the kind of man who people easily liked and trusted. He had no pretensions, and was what some people call the strong, silent type.

As kids, we loved to play with Daddy, to have him toss us in the air, or to sit on his lap. He could play guitar and harmonica, and we would often beg him to play and sing for us, such songs as Red River Valley, or The Little Brown Church in the Vale. He was a simple man with an enormous curiosity about the world, and he always provided a steady stream of magazines and books, on many subjects, for family reading material in our home. He was a great father, a reliable provider, a loving and supportive husband, and an excellent man.

I adore my Dad! He is the basis for my personal Ideal Man. This book is dedicated to him, and his picture is on the dedication page, in case you missed it.

If you did not have the advantage of an excellent father, you may not intrinsically know how to recognize good men, because they are simply unfamiliar to you. We are subconsciously more aware of things that are familiar, and they influence what we see in the world around us. For example, recently, my husband, Dixon, bought a Prius. Before he bought it, I couldn't even identify one, and surely didn't notice them on the highway. Now that we have a Prius, I see them everywhere! My brain is tuned to recognize the now-familiar shape of a Prius.

It is the same with good men. If you don't know how to recognize them, you won't even see them. Instead, you will just see the negative types of men you observed in your childhood. Or you will tune in to the types of men that Hollywood portrays, with their surface good looks. You won't know how to look more deeply.

Over the years, as I tried to find a way to describe good men, like my Dad, the image of a Gorilla came to my mind. Like my Dad, Gorillas are strong, tactile and form loyal family groups. When I used this animal concept to describe men, it seemed women were able to think in more objective terms about men.

When I married my husband, Dixon, who is not a Gorilla, he wanted to know what animal type I would label him. Dixon is handsome, and yet he tends to isolate, rather than be tactile and form family groups. He is also very artistic, and the aesthetics of his environment and appearance are important to him. In my mind, I saw a sleek panther gliding through the jungle alone. We decided he is a Panther.

Over time, more of my single female friends wanted to hear about this Man-imal concept, so I gradually developed the 12 Man-imal Types, and The Gorilla Quiz. Since then, I've gathered a following of people from all walks of life, and many countries, who are seeking to build better relationships. People have told me the Man-imal concept is approachable and a lot of fun, and it has proven itself time and again.

## The 12 Man-imal Types

Each of the 12 Man-imal Types is characterized by his focus in life. What motivates and drives him? What makes him feel like a success? Our culture is already familiar with using animal names to describe some types of men, based on their focus or their behavior. For example, you've probably heard the term "Shark" used to describe a man motivated by financial success.

And you've probably also heard a man who is focused on sexual conquests, called a "Wolf." These are two of my 12 Man-imal Types.

You can go to my website at www.GorillaLove.com to take the Gorilla Quiz and identify the Man-imal Type of any man in your life. I also recommend you take the Quiz to identify your imaginary Ideal Man. The Quiz is free and you can take it as many times as you like. If you can't get to a computer, I put a copy of The Gorilla Quiz at the end of this book.

Many relationship books describe men as if they are all the same, i.e. from the same planet. Some books give a set of Rules that are supposed to apply to all men equally. However, I believe there are many different types of men. Each man is complex, and no single set of guidelines is going to tell you how to relate to all of them. My 12 Basic Man-imal Types can combine into a myriad of unique profiles, because every man is truly a combination of Man-imal Types. Let's start by learning about the 12 basic Types.

# *The Wolf*

*His Focus is Sexual Conquests*

The Wolf's self-esteem is based on the number of his sexual conquests. The more conquests, the more he assures himself (and others) that he's a real man. Think of Hugh Hefner. This is the guy who's bragging in the locker room (or in Playboy). He's also the one who "can't keep it in his pants." And he's often the one who gets hit with sexual harassment charges and can't understand why; because all he was doing was telling a little joke or touching a woman to comfort her, etc. He honestly believes that every woman wants his attentions, so how could it be harassment?

A handsome Wolf has likely learned to be charming. He is especially good at making a woman feel she is beautiful and desirable (because in the moment he is focused on her, she is the most beautiful woman in the world to him). Therefore, as long as you can remember it's a numbers game to him, you can bask in the light of his (temporary) affection. If you want to prolong the "game," just remember this is the guy who created the need for games about "playing hard to get," so don't be easy!

Stereotypically Latin men tend to behave as Wolves; hence the term "Latin Lover." They tend to measure their virility by the number of their conquests. What is amazing to me is how many Latin women seem to think their man's cheating behavior, or even taking up a full time mistress, is okay. *What's up with that?*

Be careful, because if you fall for a Wolf and imagine you can make him love you (and you alone), you may be in for a huge heartbreak. The emotionally immature Wolf is the world's greatest heartbreaker. It feels SO good to have his focused attention, but the letdown can be huge.

Unfortunately, some women think there is something wrong with themselves when they can't keep him devoted and faithful (think Marilyn Monroe and John F. Kennedy). Nope, it's just his Wolf nature.

Even when a Wolf truly loves his wife, if he is emotionally immature, he is constantly looking at other women, undressing them in his mind, and imagining them in bed. It's like a drug that he is addicted to. It's always the next woman that he has to have to reassure him (if only to himself) that he's still "got it." You may imagine that if you are a great lover, with the best sexual techniques, you can satisfy him. But, it's not really the sex he wants, it's the thrill and the chase of the next conquest.

When a man is focused on a childish need to satisfy all his impulses and desires, he will be unable to resist temptations. Think about several of our presidents, while in the White House, unable to control their own self-serving behavior, or an array of male celebrities who have been exposed as serial womanizers.

If your Wolf really WANTS to change, you may be able to help him grow emotionally. Sometimes when a Wolf really feels the pain his cheating has caused, then he may change his behavior – *if* he is able to find real value in himself for his other qualities (which you may need to help him see). Then he will not need to constantly reassure himself with new sexual conquests.

Instead, he will be receiving positive motivation and feedback from you. You can measure his emotional growth by his ability to move away from being self-centered, toward having empathy and understanding for others (particularly you).

This may allow him to build longer-term relationships. He can get his self-esteem from the love he receives from you, although he may always have a wandering eye.

The Wolf can set the *most* romantic scene, with flowers, intimate dinners, or handholding walks on the beach. He can zero in on your greatest fantasies and play them out for you. That can be great fun and a real boost to your morale. Therefore, an emotionally mature Wolf can be a fabulous mate!

If you see Wolf behavior in someone you love, you may want to also take my Maturity Quiz about your man.

# The Pit Bull

*His Focus is Power & Control*

Of all the Man-imal types, the Pit Bull can be one of two extremes. Either he is the most loyal and protective…. or the most dangerous.

If the Pit Bull is emotionally immature, he may actually believe he "owns" his woman. He sees her as a possession, not a person. He does not believe she has a right to her own feelings, opinions, and goals—therefore he believes it is his right to tell her what to do, where she can go, what to wear, and what she may say. If she "disobeys" him, he may believe he has the right to punish her.

Think of Ike Turner (former husband of Tina Turner) for an example of a Pit Bull in the public eye. Another example is Patrick Bergin's character in the movie "Sleeping with the Enemy." Some Middle Eastern cultures support this attitude toward women as a group.

It can be especially dangerous when a woman tries to leave or divorce an emotionally immature Pit Bull, because he still believes he owns her. Sometimes he will take the position: "if I can't have her, then no one can." This is when a woman finds it necessary to file restraining orders to keep him away. But from his self-centered perspective, he cannot see that she has a right to separate from him. In fact, he may feel that she has publicly humiliated him by pulling away—and therefore she deserves to be punished, so that he can save face. He hasn't developed the mature quality of empathy to enable him to see anything from her perspective.

So why would a woman choose a man with this immature nature? Initially, it may seem romantic and loving to have a man provide everything, and take great interest in her—she may see him as a strong protector. She may even misinterpret his controlling ways as a sign of his love for her, because HE believes it is love. When he tells her what to wear, or say, or do, he thinks he is taking care of her—and initially she may also believe it's simply his way of showing love.

But it's an illusion of safety, and ultimately a trap which will get tighter and tighter. Sometimes an immature Pit Bull will set specific restrictions on his girlfriend or wife, such as imposing curfews, curtailing privacy, or setting dress codes, believing that the woman is not his equal and therefore she does not have a right to manage her own life. Or, in the guise of taking care of her, he may insist on controlling all the finances. Eventually, when she wants to make a decision for herself, he will criticize or ridicule her, or even physically hurt her to maintain his control.

To determine the emotional maturity of a man, pay close attention to how well he listens to your feelings. If he discounts or ignores what you say, then beware. For example, if you say you are uncomfortable with how fast he is driving, and he responds by saying something like, "Don't worry, I'm a good driver," then he is not listening to your feelings. Or if he insists that you will like a new food, yet when you tell him you don't even want to try it, he ridicules you—then he is ignoring your right to choose for yourself. (Big hint: Beware any man who ridicules you in any way. He is trying to control you!)

On the other hand, an emotionally mature Pit Bull can be a great mate and leader. Through his emotional maturity, he has developed the ability to empathize with people, he can relate to their wants and needs, and see things from a perspective outside his own. He adapts his need to control toward motivating others instead, maybe through enabling them to provide for their own wants and needs.

For example, a company manager may offer bonuses or promotions. A politician may promise reduced taxes or more freedoms. Therefore, people may choose to follow his leadership. As long as Pit Bull leaders stay connected with their people, they can foster a positive environment of loyal followers. However, if the Pit Bull loses his connection to others (the ability to empathize and relate), his need to control can become oppressive and foster resentment instead.

The same is true between a man and a woman. If he is emotionally mature, he will be able to listen to her and relate to her wants and needs. Because he understands her, he will find ways to fulfill her desires, and she will allow him to lead. This is especially true for women who have a dependent nature and want to have a man in charge. For these women it is important to find a man with at least some Pit Bull aspects—and the emotional maturity to be appropriate mates.

However, a woman who is strongly independent should be careful *not* to choose a Pit Bull as a partner, because her need for independence will surface and cause friction, even when her desires are being met!

# The Shark

*His focus is Financial Success*

A Shark's main focus is financial success and accumulation of status objects. The bumper sticker that proclaims: "He who dies with the most toys, wins" is probably found on the rear of a vehicle driven by a Shark.

At his worst (when emotionally immature), a Shark's greed can cause him to be selfish and deceitful in business. For example, when you hear about the destruction of the rain forest to suit the "needs" of a big business, be assured that the CEO of that business is an immature, self-centered Shark. Or when you hear about the CEO of a bank who makes $18 million a year, but lays off employees in the name of the company's need for fiscal conservation, you are seeing a Shark at his most selfish. He is literally taking the food off the table of hundreds or even thousands of employees, while filling his own pockets.

An immature Shark will ignore his lack of empathy for others by telling himself he "deserves" the best because he is better (or works harder, or takes more chances) than others. He can be self-aggrandizing and even arrogant about it. He tells himself he is nothing like those "small guys" who don't earn what he does.

On a smaller scale, you will also find Shark behavior behind a mortgage broker who adds unnecessary charges to line his own pocket. Any time that you see a man make a choice for financial gain while creating some form of loss for others, you are seeing the selfish side of a Shark. While there is nothing wrong with financial success—in fact most of us would like to enjoy more of it—it is the extent to which a man will go to gain it, at the expense of someone else, that determines the degree of emotionally immature Shark in him.

Here is a true story:

One of our friends was married to a man who was primarily a combination of Owl and Lion. This man was mostly gentle and considerate of others. But his Shark aspect took shape in the form of hanging onto money, and it drove a wedge into their marriage. He made excuses for not buying her gifts for her birthday or Christmas. She felt unloved, and so sometimes she even bought her own gifts. But she hadn't fully realized the extent of his tight-fistedness until after they divorced.

He expressed his regret for how he had treated her, and gave this example of his financial withholding: When they went out for date nights, she would often express a desire to call home to check with the babysitter about the kids (this was before cell phones). He would always tell her to quit worrying, the kids are fine. But after the divorce, he admitted that he simply didn't want her to spend the quarter for the call! This is a clear-cut case of emotionally immature Shark behavior—choosing a really small amount of money over his wife's sense of security about their kids.

An emotionally immature Shark is constantly comparing himself to others, especially the visible (or even imagined) success of others. This causes his compulsive drive for still more material gain. He wants the best of everything to convince himself (and others) that he is a winner. He is filled with envy and jealousy when he sees another man with a bigger house, more expensive car, or a status watch. Not having the best causes him self-doubt, which drives him to greater heights of greed. He may become a workaholic who ignores the need for connection with his family. He may even lie to himself and say he's working for his family.

When it comes to the Shark's attitude toward women, he may treat women as just another status symbol of success, and he may trade up for a new one every few years. Hence the term "trophy" wife. Think about Donald Trump.

An immature Shark may be so self-centered that he is unable to deeply relate to another person at all. He may not feel real empathy or connection, or prioritize someone else's needs anywhere near his own. But some really ambitious women don't care, and are willing to fake orgasms with Sharks to access a high-end lifestyle. Some are even okay with the "trading up" aspect because they look forward to a good divorce settlement for their trouble.

As we mentioned before, all the Man-imals have potential for expressing a positive side or a negative side. This is primarily dependent upon how emotionally mature he is. Infants and toddlers are totally selfish and self-focused. Their world is small and filling their own needs is paramount. By the time they reach kindergarten, most children have learned to share to some extent, or relate to and care about others.

When a Shark matures past the "me-me-me" toddler stage, and learns to balance his wants with those of others around him, he can be a wonderful man. Most women want financial security, so Sharks can be very attractive. If you want the "beautiful things" and a great life-style, it's good to find a man with some Shark tendencies, because he has the drive and ambition to create the good life. Just be sure to observe whether he is driven by a selfish need to excel or by a more emotionally mature and balanced desire for success.

# The Rhino

*His focus is his Body Image*

It is good to have a man with at least some Rhino, because he takes good care of his body and maintains a healthy lifestyle. He may also provide inspiration, or at least a harmoniously shared set of interests, for you to maintain a healthy lifestyle, too. Or maybe you just love the uber-masculine look of all those muscles, and the sense of his strength. As with all the Man-imal types, your enjoyment of him is going to be somewhat dependent upon his balance between selfish narcissism and the emotional maturity to get beyond the imbalance of self-centeredness.

Self-centered Rhinos worship their own body and imagine that everyone else does too. After all they've worked really hard, spent lots of hours, effort and money to build that body—and they're proud of it. Bodybuilding, or at least intense fitness, has been their focus for years. We're not talking about a gorgeous body like David Beckham's, who we hear is focused on his family, and also happens to be a professional athlete. No, we mean the guy who is consumed with exaggerated musculature and image. Think Vin Diesel or The Rock.

Of course, a Rhino is taking things too far and is out of balance when he uses steroids or other unhealthy or illegal substances to enhance his body.

To the Rhino, though, it's an art form to "sculpt" the muscles. In fact, since they think every man wants the body they have, they often lack respect for men who don't put in the time and energy to build up their own bodies. Rhinos really don't "get it" that some men (and many women) don't like that over-built muscle-magazine look.

Ah, but some women do! To those women, muscles are a symbol of all that is masculine. They see a "big guy" as their protector. But, if the Rhino is emotionally immature, he is focused on himself, not on protecting a woman and her feelings.

Like the Shark, a Rhino usually prefers a trophy woman on his arm. He likes the exaggerated image of a woman because it matches his exaggerated image of a man. He may prefer idealized women, who look like Barbie Dolls or Playmates.

Unfortunately, if he is on the emotionally immature end of the spectrum, his self-focus will make it unlikely that he can really connect with a woman and her feelings and needs. He can't resist looking at himself as he passes a store window.

Think Arnold Swarzenegger. Nope, you can't be a great lover when you don't deeply connect with anyone but yourself.

# The Panther

*His focus is Artistic Expression*

It's been said that a woman's best accessory is a well-dressed man. And no Man-imal does it better than a Panther!

Somewhere in his youth, he probably became aware of getting appreciation from others for his good looks. Now, he expresses his artistic nature through his appearance, so that he can continue to receive that positive feedback. Most Panthers are born good-looking and then use their gifts of artistry to enhance their appearance, so many women find them attractive. Think of George Clooney, a "classic-style" Panther. We've never seen a picture of him where he wasn't perfectly dressed for the occasion, whether it was for casual or formal activities—and no man wears a tux better on Oscar night!

While many other men are a walking fashion faux-pas, the Panther uses clothing like an artist's paint brush. He is ready, willing and able to make a fashion statement. A trendsetter, he was probably the first among his crowd to wear a plaid tie with a striped shirt, first to wear a pink shirt, or first to wear the more pointed toe shoes currently in fashion.

Because he is willing to experiment with new looks, he may purchase numerous clothing items to try, discover that he is not comfortable wearing them, and reject them. If he is emotionally immature, his self-centered need for more and more clothing options can be so strong that it overwhelms the budget. This can get expensive!

All the jokes that have been told about women—those who try on five different outfits before going out for the evening—can be told about a Panther. He will experiment endlessly with numerous different looks until he finds something that feels both comfortable and unique. The last thing he wants to do is blend in with the crowd. But he also doesn't want to stand out so far that he becomes uncomfortable.

However, for some Panthers, especially those in the public spotlight, their desire for attention may drive them to go so far that they almost appear to be wearing costumes. Think of Johnny Depp and his multiple accessories. Or similarly, a Panther may go overboard with his own unique style, such as George Hamilton and his tan.

Surprisingly, sometimes a Panther will become self- conscious about his good looks and try to hide it under a less attractive style. In this case, he uses his Panther awareness of appearance to choose looks that downplay his handsome self. Think of Brad Pitt in some of his grungy incarnations.

Although your Panther may be confident about his good looks, it's possible he actually has low self-esteem and uses his appearance to divert attention away from his tender inner self. Sometimes attractive children are emotionally damaged because everyone gives them attention for their beauty, while ignoring the person behind the pretty face. This can be doubly true for handsome gay men.

In a desire to appear cool and sophisticated, (or to protect his emotional vulnerability) some Panthers keep themselves slightly aloof from others, and thus it may be hard for them to connect emotionally.

A tendency to isolate may also be observed in the sports a Panther chooses. He may prefer individual sports, such as running, biking, or skiing. Take note if he shies away entirely from sports that put him in a situation where he must be involved with a group, i.e.: volleyball, soccer, basketball, or a casual game of football.

When it comes to career choices, Panthers seem to be more sensitive than other men to their emotional work environment. This may cause him to isolate from situations that cause him anxiety, such as careers involving lots of group interaction or potential conflict.

His aesthetic sensitivity to his physical environment can lead Panthers toward artistic careers, such as architecture, interior design, or visual marketing. It can be wonderful to have a Panther's help in improving the aesthetics of your life.

I know a Panther whose generous desire to make the environment more beautiful causes him to carry a large plastic bag on his morning walk. He uses it to pick up litter from the neighborhood. (This could also be a Lion trait.)

Although nearly all women are attracted to a Panther's good looks, some nurturing-type women can sense the wounded child within him, and feel a desire to rescue this handsome man. As with all the Man-imal types, the better you know him, the better you can understand him and work to build a relationship.

So, if you can get past his pretty face and connect with a mature Panther on an emotional level, the only negatives I know for being with him, are the aforementioned budget considerations, and the real possibility of being "lost in the crowd" yourself while everyone fawns over your man. Otherwise, enjoy your good looking Panther!

# The Monkey

*His focus is Adventure & Excitement*

Monkeys are curious about life; when young, he probably "got into everything." Sometimes Monkeys respond to parental guidance through rebellion, which can lead him into experimenting with truly dangerous aspects of life, such as drugs or street life. Of course this is alarming to parents!

However, the more you try to control a Monkey, the more he will resist. Some types of young Man-imals may listen to reason, and learn from others mistakes, but a Monkey learns by doing. He's just got to touch that hot stove to see what it really feels like.

Depending on where he grew up, his adventure seeking can take different forms. If he grew up on a farm, he might become a bull rider in rodeos. If he lives in Los Angeles, he might become a stunt actor. Or, as a teenager in Middle America, he may play in a garage band and become the next rock star.

A Monkey is always ready to try something new, often things that might seem somewhat challenging or even dangerous to the rest of us. It's as though he has no fear, wants to live life fully— and doesn't want to miss anything. He wants to bungee jump, parachute out of planes, and ride the zip-line. Excitement is like a drug that his body craves; he is a true adrenaline junkie.

For some women, this "dangerous" energy can be attractive. It can be fun and exciting to be with a Monkey. Especially if he's a "bad boy" with a tender heart of gold! In the movies this role would be played by James Dean or Marlon Brando; and how about John Travolta in Grease? Sandy just couldn't resist that exciting Monkey!

If you like your Monkey excitement to be packaged with more sophistication, think of James Bond, the classic risk-taker in a tux, with a British accent. Yum, yum!

Consider too, if you love him and are afraid he might get hurt, a Monkey's risky behavior can prove anxiety producing. An emotionally immature Monkey can go too far, always wanting to give life a little more "juice." He will selfishly pursue his "adrenaline addiction," and be oblivious to the effect on his loved ones.

Think of the bull riders who ride so often that they eventually break most of the bones in their body. Or how about race car drivers like Mario Andretti, or stuntman Evil Knievel? Or think of Steve Irwin, the crocodile hunter. These are all Monkeys. All of them perform for the public and get their "fix" by pushing the envelope.

Another group of performers are those on stage like Mick Jagger. The music world seems particularly rich with Monkey energy—lots of performers living on the edge. You can usually identify a Monkey by how he lives his life. Is he taking chances? Does he seem drawn toward risk? Again, you will find plenty of women who love to bask in his exciting limelight. The groupies follow musical Monkeys everywhere.

Because Monkeys are usually full of high energy, they can accomplish a great deal. If they also have a Shark aspect, they can be very bold in finding ways to earn an income. A good example would be Richard Branson, who is famous for his many pranks and hijinks along with a drive for financial success. What is less known about Richard Branson is his

Gorilla side, as shown by his choice to always work from home, so that he can be near his family.

There are also Monkeys who get their fix through financial risk. This can express as a gambler, or an investor, but it can also be a businessman who keeps "betting the farm" on his next business opportunity.

For example, my friend Marilyn is married to a Monkey. He is brilliant, and has invented numerous high value items. He is also a very hard working, self-made businessman. He loves adventure and is often in situations where his life is in danger: on the water or in the air. But his greatest risk-taking shows up when he repeatedly mortgaged the family home to finance all of his business ventures. Although Marilyn begs him not to do it, every time he ignores her pleas. He is convinced that he knows best and it will all work out. He thinks she should just trust him.

If your Monkey is immature, he will selfishly focus on fulfilling his reckless drive. On the other hand, if he is emotionally mature, and can balance his "need for speed" with consideration for your feelings, you can happily go along for an exciting ride!

# The Panda

*His focus is Fun & Friends*

Pandas can be SO fun! In general, they show a happy-go-lucky nature and are always ready to go-with-the flow. They want to play or joke around all day. Because Pandas like people, they are usually happiest in social situations. He will often be the one to gather people together for activities. This type is sometimes called a Teddy Bear, but we named them Pandas, in honor of Jack Black, the poster boy for this Man-imal Type. In some ways you could consider Pandas as junior Gorillas, because of their desire to be near people.

However, a Panda's immaturity can show up in troublesome ways, such as "frat boy" pranks, or overdoing when he wants to "party hearty." We think this is often caused by his inability to actually connect and build real relationships (unlike the Gorillas). Instead, a Panda will put on a smile and clown around to cover up his vulnerabilities.

Think of the classic picture of that one guy at the party who puts a lampshade on his head. This man is not comfortable with being himself, so he behaves in ways that distract from revealing his real self, and becomes a clown to entertain. Initially, because he is amusing and social, it may be hard to see that his behavior is selfish, but in reality he is focused only on himself and his emotionally insecure feelings. He is reassuring himself that he is acceptable by gathering laughter and attention.

The immature side of a Panda can also be seen in other inappropriate behavior. My friend Paula told me about attending a funeral with a Panda. She was totally embarrassed when he started cracking jokes. Thinking back on the situation, Paula believes he was uncomfortable with the tender emotions brought up in the funeral service. His jokes were his attempt to cover up his true feelings. Women who want to present a classy and sophisticated image should avoid immature Pandas.

It can take courage to face the challenges of building real relationships, and some Pandas would rather retreat into goof- ball antics.

On the other hand, a Panda who is emotionally mature can be a real delight and a marvelous companion. Think of a troubled Robert Downey, Jr. who has faced his challenges and matured into a wonderfully talented actor, and is still a playful Panda. Now he seems truly comfortable with himself and many women find him sexy and attractive.

# The Owl

*His focus is Cerebral Activities*

The Owl is the most intellectually oriented of the Man-imals. That doesn't mean he is the most intelligent, just that he spends a lot of time in his head. He likes to think about things and analyze them before he acts. He is not usually impulsive or emotional; rather he is intentionally rational and reasonable in his behavior. This is also true about his love life.

For example, I know an Owl, a CPA by trade, who actually did a spread sheet to decide whether or not to propose to the woman he had been dating for five years. He literally could not make a decision without this objective analysis.

Culturally, the Jewish heritage emphasizes intellectual pursuits, education and lots of thought provoking activity. Albert Einstein is an excellent example of an Owl, with some charming Gorilla tendencies. And even within the passionate artistic environment, Woody Allen's thoughtful films show his intellectual observations of human behavior.

The computer industry is a natural fit for many Owls. And most companies' Research and Development departments are filled with Owls, who love gathering data and analyzing it. They are the classic nerds, like Bill Gates.

Owls can be very attractive to some women. Think of Marilyn Monroe's attraction to the screen writer Arthur Miller, to whom she was married for five years. On the big screen, many women find Leonardo DiCaprio, a thinking man's actor, very attractive. And on the political scene, Barack Obama shows a strong Owl focus, with his academic background and intellectual approach toward government. He is sometimes ridiculed for his use of "big words"— but it's just his Owl nature.

Some women are attracted to Owls because they seem "safe" due to their "think before acting" behavior. This can feel like a calm sanctuary, especially for women who have been physically or emotionally abused by violent men in the past. And of course, women who are intellectually inclined enjoy the company of a man who can share stimulating conversations, or book, film, and theatre reviews.

Women who have achieved corporate success of their own are also often drawn toward men who are well-educated and can form a sophisticated couple to share objectives of moving up the career ladders.

As always, the emotional maturity of the man is the determining factor. If he is still immature and self-centered, he may not have developed the social skills to relate well with others. He may become withdrawn, detached or overly analytical about things that have emotional consequences. On the other hand, a mature Owl has depth, not just surface appeal, which can last through the years.

# The Lion

*His focus is Good Works*

A Lion is one of the nice guys. He wants to improve the world. He doesn't just think about it; he actually does something with his drive. He may choose a favorite cause and work hard to support it, such as the men who led a local environmental campaign, or camped out on behalf of Occupy Wall Street. Or he might have volunteered to serve for a few years in the Peace Corps or joined the military to defend freedoms all over the world.

A Lion may have experienced some kind of loss, and now his altruistic side leads him to work hard to improve the situation, so that no one else has the same negative experience.

On the other hand, sometimes a Lion has already achieved in some other part of his life, such as financial or political success, and now he feels a drive to do something for others. Think of Bill Gates and his support of world education—or Al Gore and his efforts for climate change.

The Lion is a believer! Although you may not agree with a Lion's agenda, in his mind he is doing something good. His ideals may be based in a particular religion; any sect from pacifist Mennonites to Islamic Jihadists. At his worst, he may selfishly believe he has the only correct answers to the world's problems, and may believe he has the right to push it on you. In such a case he has become a zealot, and will ignore your right to a different opinion. This is the emotionally immature side of Lions.

Some women are repelled by Lions, whose idealism may seem self-righteous, or his idealistic vision lacking in connection with the "real" world. A Lion's willingness to serve others may appear as a weakness to some women.

But when a Lion is open-minded and can experience empathy for others beliefs, he can be the gentlest and most understanding of all the Man-imals. He can be a true gentleman, with a kind heart toward all mankind. This requires a certain kind of strength. Think of the Dalai Lama, who offers respect to his enemies. Or think of Pope Francis. Both have devoted their lives to serving others in this world as spiritual leaders, and Lions can usually be found in other visible service roles.

When in a relationship with a man who is primarily a Lion, you may realize that his "mission" comes first, and you come second. For some women, this is good, because she too supports the mission and admires her man for his devotion to good works. In fact, for some women, their first requirement is to find a man of her same religious or altruistic persuasion.

On the other hand, for a woman who is in a relationship with a man whose profile initially shows only a small percentage of Lion, and her man experiences some kind of epiphany and then shifts his focus more completely as a Lion, it can be extremely difficult. This is especially true if she does not share his passion for his new cause in life... or even disagrees with his position outright. His new focus could be anything from a religious conversion to a conviction that Amway is the only way to create a nice lifestyle for the two of them. And sometimes new converts are particularly pushy about their new focus in life. Whew!

This can be a very tough situation and requires the use of some of the specialized communication skills presented later in this book, to save the relationship.

Alternatively, some Man-imals just gently grow the Lion aspect of their overall profile when they discover a cause that has meaning for them, or develop more time to invest in community or social causes as they mature. This is much easier for most women to handle.

# The Gorilla

*His focus is Relationships*

When you hear someone say, "He's such a sweetheart," they are probably talking about a Gorilla. They are easy-going, loving and accepting of the people around them. Gorillas connect with other people. They are observant of others' feelings and therefore don't usually make negative comments. Although they might see a "flaw" or two in their woman, Gorillas accept her as she is, and love her anyway—without mentioning such things to her.

The central characteristic of Gorillas is they are very tactile, and these men like to cuddle and touch. You are seeing "Gorilla action" when you see a man carrying a child in one arm while using the other hand to hold hands with his woman. Think Matt Damon, Patrick Dempsey and Howie Long.

Children easily recognize Gorillas, and will go to them readily, because they feel safe and secure. When you look across a crowd at the beach or park, if you see children crawling across the lap of a man, and he's totally comfortable with it, you can almost guarantee he's a Gorilla.

In general, Gorillas are not particularly verbal, more the strong and silent type. They are not prone to talking about feelings, but will be the first one to put an arm around someone who is suffering. Of the five love languages in Gary Chapman's book of the same name, a Gorilla uses "touch" to comfort and connect. That's one reason Gorillas make such great lovers.

In bed, Gorillas listen to a woman and they will remember what she likes. For example, they notice when her breathing changes and they will remember what they did to cause that change. They want her to have a good time and they will see to it that she achieves orgasm before they do—at least once, or twice! A Wolf may do the same thing, but it's just to be sure she will be available the next time he calls. A Wolf is focused on what he can get. But a

Gorilla is focused on what he is giving. He does it because it makes him happy to see her happy.

In most Nora Roberts or Shannon Stacey romance novels, the leading man is a Gorilla or has very strong Gorilla tendencies.

Most Gorillas have emotionally grown beyond the toddler stage of "me, me, me" and been able to mature into being sharing and considerate of others. They are not self-focused or narcissistic. It is this emotional maturity that is necessary for a truly loving relationship, with equal rights and responsibilities. So, no matter what Man-imal type is your favorite, look for a good percentage of Gorilla, so that your man can connect with you and together you can build a satisfying future.

Here is a true story about a friend of mine.

Gloria read the Man-imal information on my website, and then she called to tell me, "If I had known what I just learned on your website, I could still be with the love of my life."

"Oh," I said, "what did you learn?"

Gloria told me she had been with her man for eight years. During that time, she felt loved and happy... with one exception. This exception was the cause of numerous disagreements. Gloria is a very successful woman. She is a published author of four books and an international speaker. She wanted her man to get a better job. She wanted him to "develop himself."

But, he kept resisting. He would say things like, "Why should I stress myself? I'm happy with what I have. We have a nice house, decent cars and we go on good vacations. I just can't see the point of added stress."

Gloria thought he was making excuses and just being lazy.

So, she kept pushing him. And eventually they broke up.

She told me, "Now I understand it was just his basic Gorilla nature. If I had known that, I would have accepted him and we could still be together. All my friends liked him, too. They couldn't understand why I complained."

I asked Gloria if he is still available. She said, "No, he married someone else."

For ambitious women, the downside of a Gorilla can be he is comfortable with how things are. In general, Gorillas have little ambition beyond being comfortable and secure. They are happy with a simple life of backyard barbeques, weekend fishing trips, or Sunday football. They don't feel the drive to get a bigger house or fancy car just to impress the neighbors. And they really don't see any reason to stress themselves just to buy new furniture or a fancy suit. They are truly comfortable with themselves as they are. This can drive ambitious women crazy!

# The Crab

*His focus is Criticism*

The Crabs are the critics of the world. They avoid their fear of intimacy by pushing others away with their critical behavior.

They look for the flaws in others and then comment on them in negative ways. Here is a true story of a Crab focusing on flaws and thus pulling down his spouse:

A friend of mine had been married about two years. Cindy and her husband bought their first house and she wanted to decorate. She decided to start by wallpapering the guest bathroom. She bought expensive, designer wallpaper with a very large pattern. (Perhaps you know that a large pattern is more difficult to match at the seams and especially at the point where the beginning and end meet).

Well, Cindy worked very hard, until she was proud of how the new wallpaper installation looked. When she was finished, she was excited to call her husband to come and see. He walked into the room and slowly looked around, checking every seam. Then, looking back at the small space above the door he had just entered, he said, "Ah, that's where you finished. I can see where the pattern doesn't match."

Please notice that this critical statement was neither preceded nor followed by a mention of how well Cindy had matched all the other seams, nor how great the updated bathroom looked overall.

It's easy to imagine how disappointed and deflated Cindy felt. Hopefully it's also fairly obvious that his behavior would cause her to feel distant from him, especially when he does this sort of thing often.

Yet, some people mistakenly believe that criticism is a form of "holding high expectations" and therefore is a good way to help people achieve their best. They are misguided in thinking that criticism is a form of encouragement to do better.

Think about Simon Cowell on American Idol. There are four people on those judging panels, who all give feedback and make suggestions for possible improvements. But only one makes the contestants cry, with his blunt and direct criticism.

For example, sometimes you will hear a woman refer to her father by bitterly saying, "I was never good enough for him. No matter what I did, he always said, "You should have done better." This is not support! This is criticism and the child feels diminished, not enabled.

It would be entirely different if the parent had said, "Hey, I saw you trying really hard out there. I know it was tough and you did great. I believe that if you keep trying, someday you will win!" This could help a child believe in herself and try again, knowing she has her father's love and support even if she doesn't win. To be willing to try to do better requires that you feel some degree of confidence that you can achieve your objective, and also that you will live through the experience if you fail, thus you are willing to take the risk.

However, when giving support, be sure that you are being sincere and not giving false praise. It helps if you remember to praise the effort, not just the result.

Instead, the Crabs suck out the confidence and self-esteem of others. Sometimes this is done to increase the Crab's own self-esteem by appearing superior, especially when the criticism is given to a peer or spouse.

Behavioral therapists stress the necessity of giving positive feedback to every small step forward, not just when the final goal is achieved. They look for progress not just perfection.

Sometimes a Crab will defend his negative comments by saying, "I just want to be honest." But his passive-aggressive hostility is revealed by his lack of tact and empathy when giving "honest" feedback.

When asked, "Does this dress make me look fat?" a Crab might say, "Yeah, your butt looks really big." But a man with common sense and tact might say, "I've seen you in other dresses that are more flattering." There is a world of difference between the effect of these two statements!

A subtle but damaging way some Crabs criticize is by "correcting" someone else in front of others. For example, at a party, the wife may start to tell a funny story about her recent traffic accident. But at numerous points in the story, her husband corrects her: "No, the car slid only five feet not fifty," or "It's only a small scratch, not really a dent," etc.

Rather than just being resentful at a Crab's criticism, it's helpful to realize that Crab behavior is a defense mechanism. It is a cover-up for the vulnerable man inside. It is not true Man-imal behavior. Most likely the Crab was raised by a Crab parent, and learned negative responses to defend himself. I feel true compassion for Crabs' painful childhoods—but I don't recommend you get into a relationship with one!

True story:

I know a woman who married a Crab, although I (and several others) warned her to stay away. But Catherine felt this man had many redeeming qualities underneath, and in spite of his Crab behavior, he was the right man for her. Before she married him, Catherine got him to acknowledge he had a critical focus and he agreed he would change it.

Together, over the years, they worked on it— but this is a very hard habit to break! Catherine and both of their children were often on the receiving end of his flaw-finding temper (though there was never physical abuse).

Fifteen years into the marriage they were still battling with his negativity. (Remember this is a man who stated he actively wanted to change, and he worked at it!) He had improved some and we could all see some of the underlying man, worthy of her commitment.

But then Catherine started to see some of the same critical and angry responses in their teenage son. This motivated the parents to work even harder and so they attended a personal growth workshop together. In the workshop, the husband made a huge breakthrough. With a great deal of courageous self-honesty, he was able to let go of the shell of criticism he had built to protect himself. Now, 19 years into the marriage, we can all see the tender and playful Panda underneath the Crab she married!

This highly unusual woman had the vision and the strength to stick with her man and support him through the trials of his personal growth. And this courageous Crab was truly willing to acknowledge his critical behavior pattern was damaging his family relationships. Catherine asked me to include her story to give hope to any woman in a similar situation.

However, I observed this woman as she faced her challenges, and I've got to say I couldn't have stuck with him. Of course Catherine was in love with him, and surely that helped her stay with him while he matured.

When you take The Gorilla Quiz, be sure to note how much Crab your man has. I suggest you also take the Quiz about your father, to see if he has a similar critical pattern. Even though we don't want to, we often marry someone with similar negative patterns.

# The Rat

*His focus is Blaming Others*

Rats rarely take ownership or accountability for their own behavior and the results they create. To them, their misfortune is always someone else's fault.

As a child, he said he got a D grade because "the teacher didn't like him," or "she wasn't fair." Later, he lost his job because "the supervisor has it in for him." He can't get a raise because "the boss is a racial bigot." He can't afford a house because "the banks are run by the corrupt government," etc.

Rats are the losers and criminals of the world. The prisons are full of men who "didn't do it." Even if they did, it was "the other guy's fault." The other guy started the fight. The other guy "had it coming." The woman they beat was "asking for it."

Unlike the approach taught in Twelve Step programs, where you first have to acknowledge who you are (i.e. I am an alcoholic), before you can move toward who you want to be, the Rats refuse to acknowledge who they are in their own lives, and instead focus on blaming others for shortcomings or disappointments. In doing so, Rats give up their own power and place themselves in a constant "victim" position.

Like the Crab, a Rat is not really a Man-imal in his core temperament. It is his compensating survival mechanism learned in childhood to cope with challenges he faced. This victim mentality is an extremely difficult position to overcome. In general, I would suggest you run like hell if your man has much of this quality!

If you decide to stay with a high-scoring Rat (above 5 points), it will take a LOT of work to help him release his victim position—because he believes it's really true! He will fight you (and blame you) every step of the way as he wrestles with his own demons. It is very painful for him to acknowledge his own mistakes and weaknesses. It takes a great deal of courage for a Rat to face the fact that his own behavior has created his poor results.

Even if he receives actual discrimination, it is still a more powerful position to ask himself, "Given this, what can I do to change my results?"

If your man is willing to move toward change (and HE has to really WANT to change) it's not enough that you want him to change! He will need abundant recognition from you for every small step forward he takes, no matter how tiny. You will need to supply consistent support and understanding even when he falls back into his old blaming "victim" position. Even professional therapists have a hard time helping someone release their blaming behavior.

Somewhere underneath his Rat behavior is the real man and his natural temperament and desires, but it's hard to see unless he sheds his Rat attitude.

I want to caution you to check your own motives if you choose to get involved with a Rat. Are you addicted to being a "rescuer?" Do you imagine yourself in a Mother Teresa role, where people are going to praise your self-sacrificing behavior? I suggest you carefully read the section on boundaries in this book.

# After the Quizzes

I'm hoping that by now you have gone to my website (GorillaLove.com) and taken The Gorilla Quiz, at least once. When I am coaching, I ask my client to take the Gorilla Quiz about ALL the significant men in her life… and also her imaginary Ideal Man. I gather the results for each one, then I put all the information on a spread sheet, like this:

|          | Ideal Man | Dad | Sam | Max | Frank | Tony |
|----------|-----------|-----|-----|-----|-------|------|
| Wolf     | 3         | 1   | 6   | 4   | 5     | 2    |
| Pit Bull | 2         | 11  | 2   | 3   | 1     | 4    |
| Shark    | 4         | 10  | 6   | 5   | 4     | 8    |
| Rhino    | 9         | 4   | 2   | 10  | 5     | 6    |
| Panther  | 7         | 6   | 5   | 8   | 7     | 4    |
| Monkey   | 8         | 6   | 0   | 2   | 4     | 3    |
| Panda    | 9         | 9   | 10  | 8   | 9     | 11   |
| Owl      | 10        | 7   | 2   | 11  | 6     | 4    |

Your Ideal Man and The 12 Man-imals

| | | | | | | |
|---|---|---|---|---|---|---|
| Lion | 8 | 10 | 0 | 10 | 3 | 6 |
| Gorilla | 14 | 7 | 8 | 13 | 10 | 9 |
| Crab | 0 | 13 | 2 | 0 | 2 | 3 |
| Rat | 0 | 11 | 7 | 1 | 0 | 1 |
| Total | 74 | 95 | 50 | 75 | 56 | 61 |
| Maturity Quiz | 92 | 48 | 41.5 | 74 | 68 | 52 |

Next, I analyze the results and highlight the highest scores. Most of the above spreadsheet is taken from Sarah's actual Quiz results.

First, I look at what Sarah wants for her Ideal Man. When you look at the above spreadsheet you will see Sarah prefers a combination of intellectual Owl and cuddly Gorilla.

Then, I look to see if there is a pattern in the men's Crab and Rat scores, because of their strong negative impact. You can see that Sarah's father scored very high in both Crab and Rat, but Sarah has managed to mostly avoid those characteristics in the men she dates. Good for Sarah!

After that, I look to see if there are other noticeable patterns in the men Sarah has allowed into her life. The first thing you'll see in her example is a lot of cuddly Gorilla and social Panda. These men help Sarah feel accepted, since her self-esteem is fairly low due to the negative impact her father's critical Crab and blaming Rat qualities had in her life.

And, you can see, even though Owl is one of the two Man- imal types Sarah prefers, only one man in her life scored high in Owl.

Finally, I check the Maturity scores. Most of the men on Sarah's spreadsheet actually scored fairly low. A score of 50 or below indicates a serious level of immature behavior and attitudes.

To help you understand the impact of maturity on the Man- imal Types, I'm going to take a few minutes to explain it.

## Emotional Maturity

All of the Man-imal Types (except Crab and Rat) can be either positive or negative, depending on their emotional maturity. Here is how I define maturity:

Imagine a horizontal scale, or continuum. On the left end is Immature and on the right is Mature.

Immature -------------------------------------Mature

Think of the most extreme immaturity as a two-year-old child; his world is totally self-centered. He has no patience, he wants what he wants—and he wants it now! He has no empathy for others, and won't share his toys. He is not interested in noticing or responding to your feelings, he just wants to cry about his own. Every child goes through this stage of development. But, most of them continue to grow and develop as they mature. Some don't.

For the man who does continue to develop and mature, it's easy to observe his ability to listen to others and understand their perspectives. He has empathy and can feel the pain of others. He is generous and willing to share. And, one of the hallmarks of maturity is that he can delay gratification.

When I speak to women's groups, I usually use male celebrities as examples for the different Man-imals, because everyone is familiar with them and their public persona. Since I don't personally know any of these men, it's entirely possible their public persona and relationship reality don't match. Maybe the tabloids exaggerate?

Anyway, for my male celebrity example, regarding emotional maturity, I usually refer to Donald Trump. I started doing so even before he became a Republican presidential candidate, which has certainly elevated his degree of visibility as of this writing. I ask my audience of women to raise their hand if they think he is mostly on the left side of the scale (immature), and then I ask for a raise of hands for those who think he is mostly on the right side (mature). The majority in every crowd perceives him as mostly immature, or self-centered. Then I ask if it is because he is a Shark and focused on financial success. Some women think "yes"—that a financial focus will make a man self-centered.

So, then I mention Bill Gates, who also has strong Shark in his profile, and who has made more money than Donald Trump ever will. Again, I ask for a raise of hands for those who see Bill Gates as immature, and then for those who see him as mature. Invariably, the audience perceives Bill Gates as more mature, probably due to his well-known, generous philanthropy and commitment to helping promote education worldwide.

Both men have a strong Shark aspect in their profile, but they are entirely different expressions of this trait due to their emotional maturity level.

Sometimes women tell me there seems to be an increase in the number of immature/self-centered men. There are many theories about the cause. At the bottom line, it is important for women to recognize both the signs of emotional immaturity as well as the benefits of a high maturity level.

# Is Your Man Self-Centered and Childish?

Sometimes we love our man, but he just drives us crazy! This may be because he is emotionally immature. Perhaps he makes plans, but doesn't follow through—like promising he'll take you out, but then says he's too tired. When you try to discuss something that's been worrying you, does he turn it into a conversation about himself? When it's your birthday, does he give you a lame excuse about having no money... when you know he just bought himself an expensive toy? Or, maybe he says he'll meet you at a certain time, but he's usually late? Does he expect you to clean up after him, as if you are his mother?

All of these are behaviors of a man who is emotionally immature and self-centered.

When you take the Maturity Quiz, you will learn some things about your man. If his score is 50 or below (out of the possible 100), you know he is behaving in immature ways. Maybe he's tried to convince you it's your fault, by saying things such as: "If you'd quit nagging me, I'd pick up my stuff." *What?!* Or, when he mishandles his money and can't buy you a birthday present or pay for his half of the dinner, does he say, "Why are you always getting on my case about money, it's all you think about!" This type of response is an attempt to avoid accountability (Rat) by focusing the negativity on you.

Don't fall for it by trying to defend yourself! Instead, you might say, "We are not talking about me at this moment, we're talking about you and how you handle your money."

But the real question is…. are you willing to put up with his childish and self-centered behavior, even if he never changes?

When you continue to allow emotionally immature behavior (although you may be verbally complaining or attempting to have discussions about it), but nothing changes, you are sending a message that it's acceptable. You are actually enabling his immature behaviors to continue! So again, ask yourself, can I allow this behavior? If your answer is "yes"—quit complaining about it, even silently.

If, on the other hand, there is a behavior that you just can't tolerate, tell him so… then mean it! Be sure to tell him what the consequences will be if it keeps happening with no sign of his real effort to change. For example, if he keeps being late, you might want to tell him that when he is 10 minutes late, you will leave without him. And you have to stick to it! Don't wait an extra couple minutes! If you don't maintain the boundary you have set, he won't respect it.

So whenever you are frustrated with someone's immature or self-centered behavior, ask yourself if you are willing to continue allowing it. Setting boundaries and maintaining them is your responsibility. It's a form of self-care and self-respect. Healthy boundaries create healthy relationships. (more about boundaries in a future chapter)

Just so you know, if you brought up some of these issues with a man who is emotionally mature, he might say, "Okay, hon, I can see that's a problem, so I'll work on it." And then you would see him actually make some real efforts to change.

## Sarah Does the Quizzes

When Sarah did the quizzes, we saw she had been doing a good job of avoiding some of the things she didn't like in her father; the over-controlling Pit Bull and negative Crab/Rat aspects of his profile. However, overall her men's scores were fairly low in Maturity.

She hadn't been clear about how to recognize what she wants. Learning to *recognize* what you want is the key, because I believe there are enough good men for those of us who know enough to choose them. We just don't recognize them when we see them. Instead we are looking at the surface things, attributes like six-pack abs, or GQ clothing. The Gorilla Quiz helps women look deeper for what they really want in a man.

Sarah and I talked at length about the difference between what she wants and what she had been getting. Previously, it had not occurred to her that she has a desire for the intellectual conversation of an Owl. Sarah is actually a fairly deep person who loves philosophical and psychological discussion. Previously she has fulfilled this need only through her female friends, but now she realized she wants this in her future male companions, as well. And she wants an emotionally mature Gorilla, not just a cuddly one.

Now that Sarah was crystal clear about the type of man she wants, she was ready to move on to the next step in my Gorilla Coaching.

Remember, you can take The Gorilla Quiz for FREE by visiting my website at GorillaLove.com. You can use this book to coach yourself, or feel free to email me if you would like some personalized help. I would love to hear from you! Angeline@GorillaLove.com

# Chapter 1

# Chapter 2:

# "I Can't Find Any Good Men!"

*"We come to love not by finding a perfect person, but by learning to see an imperfect person perfectly."*

—Sam Keen, To Love and Be Loved

## How to Recognize Good Men

After taking both The Gorilla Quiz and The Maturity Quiz and analyzing the results, you will be crystal clear about the type of man you want in your life. The next step is to start looking for some potential men. Yay! Scary! Confusing? Maybe you're thinking, "That's just the problem. I don't know where to find any good men."

Where have you been looking so far? On-line dating websites? Singles bars? Although it is possible to find a good man there, they are rare. Many of the men at those places are just looking for a quick hook-up. After a few disappointments with the poor quality and shallow men you find in those locations, you could mistakenly begin to believe there are no more good men.

## Where Have all the Good Men Gone?

Often I hear women say, "All the good men are taken" or "I can't find the right guy." There seems to be a general belief that all the available guys (and some of the married ones) are jerks. But, when I was dating, in my 20s and again in my 40s, I found many good men. How?

First, I think many women make the mistake of looking for perfect men. I'm sorry to tell you, but there are no perfect men. And...there are no perfect women...nor any perfect children, either. So, if you are out there looking for flaws in the men you meet, you will always find them! Because, bottom line, there are no perfect people.

Second, I think most women don't really know what they want and need in a companion. I think we have been fed a lot of baloney by the media. We are led to believe that the Ideal Man is like the current "sexiest man alive." Or we watch Magic Mike and think we should have a man with a terrific six-pack and gorgeous hair. We want a man we can show off to our friends, like a trophy we've won. Like a stamp of approval that says, "I am worth it, I'm a winner."

All this malarkey creates a shallow relationship. Those men are like cardboard characters. Those men aren't real. It's the same as men yearning after the photo shopped and silicone-enhanced Barbie dolls in Playboy magazine. Those women aren't real. When we search for a cardboard character of a man, we end up with a cardboard relationship.

Women often tell me stories of finding the "perfect" man: he's gorgeous, he works out regularly, dresses with style, has a great job, keeps his car clean, etc. All the "external" things look great. But when they want to start a relationship they find out his focus is all surface and he avoids anything deeper, such as commitment. No wonder women feel disappointed!

Third, a lot of the skills we have been taught to use, when meeting and dating men, are all about playing games, following some set of "rules" and hiding our true feelings. In short, we are told to present a false image. And this is supposed to help us find a real man and develop a real relationship? No wonder the divorce rate is so high! A few years into the relationship, both partners are saying, "You're not who I thought you were."

When you want a real relationship, it's important to be authentic. For example, imagine that you are going to the store to buy some new shoes. Perhaps your feet are large, maybe size 10, and you are embarrassed because you want to have perfect (dainty and feminine) size 7.5 feet. So you tell the clerk you are looking for shoes in size 7.5, and you buy a gorgeous pair of shoes in a size 7.5 that you're really looking forward to wearing with some of your favorite outfits.

But, when you get home and try to wear them, they don't fit, of course. They hurt, and you still persist, hobbling down the street and into the office. You were not "authentic" about who you are when you were shopping for shoes, and even though you really tried, they simply don't fit. The same is true when you go "shopping" for a man. If you are not authentic about who *you* are, then the man you find will not be a good fit for you.

And just so you don't go overboard with being authentic, there is no need for you to shop for shoes when your feet are dirty. And there's no need for you to be obnoxious and show your worst side on a date either. Just sayin!

If you were raised in a dysfunctional home (and most of us were to some extent), you probably observed some poor behavior between your parents. They may have been disrespectful or sarcastic to each other, and to you. Perhaps they were verbally or even physically abusive.

Unfortunately, this means you are carrying some negative baggage. When we are children, we don't know how to filter the behavior we observe. We don't have the knowledge of what is good and reasonable. As a child we may assume our parents are right in the ways they behave, even if we know what they are doing is not good. Even though we don't like their negative ways, we still absorb them as normal. As a little girl, if you saw your Dad, uncles, or brothers acting like jerks, it may be natural for you to believe that most men are jerks.

Think about the male behavior you observed while growing up. Can you name some specific negative attitudes or behavior you saw? Did someone treat your mother with disrespect? In what ways? Was is emotional or physical abuse? And how were you treated? Were you ridiculed as you began to show signs of womanhood? Were the women in your family treated as "less than" the men? Was there a male outside your family who treated you poorly? Maybe a neighbor or teacher? Are you one of the 25% of women who has been sexually abused?

If any of these negative behaviors happened to you, unfortunately you are now carrying those negative images of men in your emotional baggage. This makes it harder for you to find and recognize good men. Let me please acknowledge that it's unfair! It's not your fault! And my heart hurts for you! You deserve all the help and understanding you can gather for yourself to heal the baggage and re-pattern your expectations of men. I want to be part of your support system. I wrote this book to help you overcome the negative conditioning you received so unfairly!

Or, are you one of the lucky few whose family supported your hopes and dreams? Did they encourage you to believe in yourself? Were the men in your family kind and considerate to others, especially women and children? Were females treated as equals to the males? Now you really can't comprehend why you can't find a good man like Dad!

## Sarah Learns about Good Men

At this point in the Gorilla Love Coaching process, I gave Sarah an assignment to observe men behaving well, and to document it. She responded, with a doubtful tone of voice, "Like what?" She couldn't even imagine what good male behavior looks like. So I gave her some examples:

- o When you see a man carrying a baby in one arm and holding a woman's hand with the other, and he's smiling…. that is good male behavior.

- o When you see a teenage boy pushing his younger sister on the swings, while she laughs…. that's good male behavior.

- o When you see a man exiting the grocery store, carrying flowers, with a smile on his face…. that's good male behavior.

- o When you see an elderly man and woman holding hands while they walk down the street…. that's good male behavior.

- o When you see a man holding doors open for others…that's good male behavior.

- o When you see a child crying in the department store and a man is down on his knee talking patiently to the child…. that's good male behavior.

o When you see a man jogging while pushing a stroller…. that's good male behavior.

These are all examples of good, nurturing male behavior. It is important to start observing these positive behaviors. You need to know that good men exist before you will believe you can find one. If you are not used to looking for this kind of good behavior, you may have developed a blind spot and skip right over it.

Start making a note of men behaving well! Remember the Prius story? Implant those good images in your brain!

## What's His Back Story?

After you start learning to recognize good men, the next step is to look more deeply into the men that interest you.

Perhaps, like Sarah, you had an over-controlling father who did not allow you to question his behavior or to think for yourself. If this is the case, you may not realize that you should always question the men you allow into your life. You should do your "due diligence" to find out more about him.

Many years ago, people lived in small neighborhoods where it was easy to know the background of just about everyone in the community. You knew their reputation, work ethic, and values. Today, in this fast paced world, when people move every few years, with 10-minute dating, and dating profiles on global websites, it is easy for anyone to create a false image of who they really are and what they are looking for.

Pay attention to the things a man says, not just the chemistry between the two of you. I recommend you verify the things he tells you about himself.

Here are some ways I suggest you check his back story:

1. Google him. Enter his name in Google and see what comes up. Does it match the things he's told you about himself? Did you get some new information? By the way, you should Google your own name, too. What are you presenting unwittingly? Is there anything out there that someone might think is you, and isn't? Are there opportunities to be more forthcoming, or at least outgoing, that will help a man who does his own homework believe you are who you say you are?

2. Next look at his Facebook page. When I suggested this to one young woman, she responded, "Oh, but he'll know I was checking on him." That's right, he will, and

his reaction will give you additional information about him to consider, too.

If he is immature, trying to play games, or keep secrets, he may react angrily and ask, "What's the matter with you, don't you trust me?" (But trust is earned, not demanded. I will explain more about trust in Chapter 5.)

On the other hand, if he is emotionally mature, open, and honest, he may say, "I noticed you looked at my Facebook page. See anything interesting? I also looked at yours." When I described this to an attractive, single, male attorney, he said, "I would expect a woman to check on me. If she didn't, I would wonder about her lack of sophistication in today's world."

Here are some things to look for on his Facebook page:

How long has it been up? Facebook has been around a long time, and most people have a page that shows at least five years of history. If it was just recently created, does he have a logical reason why? If it's new and has very little information, I would wonder if it's based on a real person or if it's a deceptive creation.

Does it show pictures with his family? Do they look happy together? Do his family members make positive comments about him? Since most of us come from a dysfunctional family to some degree, it would be unusual for him to have a happy, "Leave it to Beaver" family. However, if there is *NO* family shown on his FB page, it probably means he is carrying some negative baggage, and he may need to do some work in order to be ready for a connected, nurturing relationship.

Does it show lots of friends enjoying each other in different activities? Do the friends look like people you would want to associate with? Or is it mostly just a bunch of guys drinking?

Does he make intelligent comments on FB? Does he post about things that interest you? Common interests aren't necessarily vital, and a mix of interests can make a relationship richer and more varied. The most important thing is to have similar *values*. Is there something that is necessary to you? For example, are you a vegan, and did you discover his profile shows him going deer hunting with his buddies? Or maybe there is a religious perspective that matters to you, or a red flag on comments he makes about another religion?

Finally, does his profile page match up with the things he told you about himself? All of these are important aspects of his life that you can learn about on Facebook, or any other social media platform.

Note: Some people have limited the information that is available to the public on Facebook, so you may not be able to see all the above unless you become his friend on the site. Even then, it's also possible that he could be selective with his friends lists, and you could still not be shown everything he does online. Be sure to continue looking in other avenues!

3. Next, look for him on LinkedIn. Did he tell you where he works? In today's business world, most people are listed on LinkedIn, so it's a good way to verify what he has told you about his career.

Again, check out the people he is connected to, and the comments they have to say about him, if any. Not everyone solicits endorsements or recommendations on LinkedIn, and especially if he has held the same job for some time, perhaps he has not been using it to attract new opportunities. It is still an insight into how he conducts himself in the workplace and whether he told you a story or the truth.

How long has he been at the same job? Does it show him getting promotions? Or does he change jobs often? Did he stay in the same industry, or switch around? Again, privacy concerns may prevail as not everyone engages in publicly visible ways through LinkedIn. Perhaps his boss would become threatened if he built up an extensive profile, or maybe he works in a business or an industry where LinkedIn is not nearly as important as face-to-face connection or word of mouth.

4. You can also look at other social media, such as Twitter, Instagram and Pinterest. What does he follow? Who follows him?

5. Go beyond social media and dig for mentions of your man. Although there is sometimes flawed data, you can also get some insight through directory searches or alumni sites for who he is, where he has lived, who his family members may be, or anything else that could verify the back story he gave you.

6. If the court case histories are searchable in the places where he lives and works, look and see if there are marriages and divorces beyond what he told you about. Is there a criminal docket, or has he been sued an unsettling number of times? It's good to learn as much as you can about a man,

before you consider allowing him into your life.

7. Meet his friends and family. What are they like? Are they the kind of people you want to be involved with for the rest of your life? How do they interact with your man? You should be able to pick up some clues about the baggage he is carrying from his childhood. Has he worked on those issues, or is he still reactive when they push his buttons?

Does all this research take away the romantic notions you have about relationship? Unfortunately, the lovely picture of just seeing someone and falling in love, and then living happily ever after is not realistic. It's one of the myths that may have allowed you to get in relationships that were unhealthy for you.

Now that you know how to recognize good men, and you know how to do your due diligence to verify the stories a man tells you about himself, you will probably find that your view of men will automatically make some changes.

## Sarah Changes her Dating Patterns

For example, within one week of this stage of the Gorilla Love process in coaching, Sarah started dating a different type of man. She had been meeting men through the Tinder dating website. Previously, she usually chose men based on their good looks. And when she went out with them, she had only paid attention to the sexual chemistry.

Now she looked deeper. After talking with a man on the phone, she would now go to Facebook and LinkedIn to verify what he said about himself. She also paid attention to the type of relationships he had with his friends and family, as shown on these websites. She could evaluate whether his profiles at least agreed with the character he portrayed to her.

Sarah even went back over the men she had previously contacted or dated via Tinder. This time she eliminated some of them based on her due diligence. She re-contacted several, who had not made an exciting initial impression, but who now appeared more interesting to her based on a deeper evaluation.

She knew her primary interests were Owl and Gorilla, so she looked for those qualities. She also knew how to look for a man with good behavior. She dated several more men, gradually choosing better and better options for herself. And in short order, she found a potential match!

A man she had dated once, but eliminated previously because he didn't seem exciting, now piqued her interest anew. They went out on a second date. She paid attention to the way he treated her. He was considerate and respectful. He listened to what she had to say, and made intelligent comments showing his interest in her life and her thoughts. He had a young son from a previous marriage, and he talked about his son with love and insight. He was also financially stable. This was a BIG change from the type of men she previously dated.

It was almost exactly four months since Sarah came to me for coaching, and Sarah felt she was falling in love with this man!

Congratulations to Sarah!

This is the ultimate goal for many dating and relationships books...to find a great guy who you love and will love you back. Many of those relationship books only guide you through the dating jungle.

But my goal for you is bigger than that! Yes, I want you to find an Ideal Man, but even more than that, I want you to have the skills you need to build a life-long Love Affair. For you, I want long-term success, not just a life of happier dating! I want you to marry a man you love, if that's what you really want—and avoid being part of the over 50% who get a divorce! So keep reading...

During coaching, Sarah and I talked a great deal about the baggage she carried from her own childhood. At this point, I surely congratulated her on her wonderful progress, but I also cautioned her that there were challenges ahead, because of the poor relationship patterns she learned as a child. She still had a lot of work to do on herself to build a strong and loving, long-term relationship with this potential Ideal Man.

For most of my clients, their first relationship challenge is learning to set and maintain healthy boundaries, so that's what I'm going to cover in the next chapter.

If you have been taking the Quizzes and following along with Sarah's journey, you are probably already seeing some of the men in your life differently, too. If you have questions, please feel free to send me an email: Angeline@GorillaLove.com.

# Chapter 3:

# "Okay, I Admit, My Boundaries are a Hot Mess!"

*"When you value yourself, unacceptable behavior is no longer acceptable."*

— Lisa D'Alessio

# Recognizing Your Boundaries

Through Gorilla Love Coaching, I see many relationship issues, and it seems a majority of them are caused by poor boundary management. Setting and maintaining healthy boundaries is usually the first skill I cover with my clients. Learning to manage boundaries is an important early step in my clients' journey, as they gain the skills they need to build long-term, loving relationships.

Because setting and maintaining healthy boundaries is so central to loving relationships, I'm going to explain boundaries from several perspectives. I want you to be super clear about your own boundaries, so you can recognize when they are out of balance or being trespassed upon by someone else.

Look at the following statements:

o   I feel so overwhelmed!

o   My account is overdrawn... again!

o   Can't believe I ate (or drank) that!

o   My sister-in-law makes me so angry!

o   My boyfriend and I are always arguing!

o   My neighbor is so rude to me!

Did you recognize that these are all boundary issues? Most people don't. Our lives get out of balance whenever we don't manage our boundaries. The first three issues are about self-management, which includes setting and maintaining boundaries with ourselves, such as scheduling regular exercise, or balancing our checkbooks, or managing our diet.

The last three examples involve managing boundaries with another person. Here is a simple definition of boundary management when it involves another person: *A boundary is a place where your space and responsibility ends and another person's begins.*

## Invisible Fences

Fences between yards make it easy to see where one property ends and the other begins. Boundaries are like invisible fences. Because they are invisible, they sometimes get crossed without awareness. Other people may not realize they are "in your space."

This is the reason it is so important for you to be super clear about knowing your own boundaries, and then to speak up and let others know about them, too. You can "speak" your fence into existence.

## Boundaries in Families

We first learn about boundaries from our families. Here are some examples of HEALTHY family boundaries.

- ○ Family members respect each other's personal space: their room, their things, and their bodies.

- ○ They speak respectfully, no ridiculing or name-calling.

- ○ They clean up their own messes.

- ○ Each is responsible for their own chores, schoolwork, and outside activities.

- o Each is accountable for their own behavior and emotional reactions.

- o They support each other's efforts.

Most families are dysfunctional to some degree. Here are some common ways that your family may have made it difficult for you to set or maintain healthy boundaries.

- o They ignore the boundaries you set.

- o They invade your space.

- o They ridicule your choices.

- o They discount your feelings.

- o They blame you for their behavior.

- o They sabotage your dreams.

- o They give you unsolicited advice.

Now that you are an adult, it is YOUR responsibility to recognize and defend your own boundaries. A lack of clear boundaries invites a lack of respect. When you allow others to manipulate you (with guilt-making, belligerence, or shaming, etc.), you are allowing them to disrespect your boundaries.

If your boundaries were constantly disrespected during your childhood, you may have become numb to boundary trespassing. So, how can you become more aware? Here is a clue: Whenever you are feeling worried, frustrated, insecure, or resentful, it's likely that your boundaries are being threatened in some way. This feeling of discomfort is a "signal" to you, to check and see if your boundaries need clarification or maintenance.

For most of us, it is scary to tell someone they are trespassing our boundary. It may involve conflict, and most of us want to avoid that. You probably want everything to be sweet and peaceful. But, when your boundaries are crossed, you are not feeling sweet and peaceful, whether or not you took the opportunity to speak up. Instead, you are probably feeling resentful if you said nothing. And the more you allow the resentment to fester, the angrier you may get, until you explode. Your man may go through the same process, too.

Or maybe you get passive-aggressive, which means on the surface you are being passive, when you are actually being aggressive underneath. For example, if he likes to be on time and he insists you go with him to football games (which you don't like), you may be passive and pretend you like football, but be slow to get ready (that's the aggressive part), so that he misses the kick off.

Obviously this is damaging to a relationship. But your fear of conflict may cause you to choose an appearance of peace, rather than speak openly about the fact that you don't enjoy football. Most of us have done something like this a time or two. It's human nature, but unproductive for relationship building.

To build healthy long-term relationships, it is always best to be authentic and say what you really feel. Of course, you can be diplomatic. You don't have to say, "It's such a stupid game. I can't believe big guys get paid millions to chase a misshaped ball. What a bunch of idiots!" Instead, you could be gracious and say, "It's just not my thing, honey. You go and have fun with the guys, while I go for a mani-pedi."

## Circles of Responsibility

There are many different ways of explaining boundaries.

One of my favorites was coined by my mother, psychologist Dr. Lorraine Manderscheid. She taught her clients about Circles of Responsibility. I'm going to share that concept with you, because I think it is very helpful in learning to understand and manage boundaries.

Picture a target.

If each of these circles represent your responsibilities, who should be in the center?

1. If you have a child, you might think your child should be in the center. This is a heartful response.

2. Some women say their man should be in the center, this is a loving response.

3. And, some say God should be in the center, which is a reverent response.

In answer to number 1 above, sorry to say, but your child is not your first responsibility. Remember the last time you were on an airplane? The crew explained the need for those traveling with children, in the event of a drop in air pressure, to put the mask on themselves first, rather than their child. Hopefully, the reason is obvious. If you become unconscious, you will be unable to take care of your child.

Number 2, regarding your man, is similar. Even though you love him, if you don't make yourself a priority by getting enough sleep, good nutrition, and mental/emotional health breaks, there will be very little to give him.

For both 1 and 2, it doesn't mean that you should be selfish and lie on the sofa and eat chocolates while your child or lover starves. It means that you need to be sure to take care of your NEEDS, before focusing on their WANTS.

As for number 3, I don't believe God is your responsibility. Instead, I believe that He will help take care of the person in your center circle...which should be you.

Putting yourself in your center circle means, fill your own basket first. If you are exhausted, from overwork, lack of sleep, or being emotionally drained, you will have little to share with those you love.

## The Fountain

And here is still another way to explain boundaries. For a different view, and more clarity—instead of looking at the circles as a target, let's look at them from the side as if they were a fountain.

When looking at the fountain, is it selfish to fill the top center cup first? No, because, as you see in the picture, when the center cup is full, it overflows to fill the others. In fact, the more you fill your own cup (perhaps from good nutrition, spiritual teachings, rest, meditation, yoga, etc.), the more it overflows to fill the next ring, and the next, and the next.

The concept of Circles of Responsibility will help you define your boundaries by clarifying your priorities. Being in the center of your circles means your first priority is self-care, such as:

o   Your physical health

o   Your personal/spiritual growth

o Your emotions and reactions (more about this in Chapter 4)

o Your social life

o Your finances

After giving yourself healthy, basic care, your responsibility extends outward to the next circles:

2$^{nd}$ Circle - Your lover, spouse, partner, etc.

3$^{rd}$ Circle - Your children (note for single moms: please see additional information about this point, at the end of this chapter)

4$^{th}$ Circle - Your employer or career

5$^{th}$ Circle - Your extended family (note: extended-family money issues come only after you secure your own financial stability)

6$^{th}$ Circle - Your community

And, if you have enough resources, time, energy, etc.... eventually your responsibility can include all peoples in the world.

Each of these circles represents a boundary. Your responsibilities gradually reduce as you move outward on the circles. The more clearly you define your circles, the easier it is to manage your priorities.

# Consequences

Perhaps you are still confused about your boundaries. Maybe you're not sure what boundaries you should set, or how to manage them or communicate them to others. One tool that may help you clarify your boundaries is to look at the consequences of not setting a boundary when needed. Let me give you some examples:

**Scenario 1. Your exercise class vs his report:** Perhaps your boyfriend needs to finish an important report for his job, and its due tomorrow morning. He is usually very good at managing his job responsibilities, including getting reports in on time. But, he wants a few hours of your help tonight, because you are an expert at Excel graphs. However, tonight is your favorite Zumba class of the week. What are the realities and possible *consequences* in this scenario?

*Reality 1:* Because he has shown a history of being responsible, it is not likely this will be an ongoing pattern of him expecting your assistance.

*Reality 2:* If you help him, you will only miss one Zumba class and can return next week.

These two realities imply consequences that are small and short-term; therefore, it would be acceptable in this case to help him. You might explain some of the finer points of Excel so that he could do it himself in the future.

**Scenario 2. Your career vs your health:** This is usually a much harder determination for my clients to make because both sides of the equation are personal. Imagine you are in a high-pressure, competitive career. You wake up with a fever of 104 and a raw throat. You know that both the flu and strep throat have been going around. You want to stay in bed! What are the realities and possible consequences?

*Reality 1:* If you go to work, you are probably spreading the sickness to your fellow employees, who are going to be frustrated with you.

*Reality 2:* But, if you love your job, and the prevailing "un-written" policy is to go to work in any condition, then you may want to suck it up and go anyway.

*Reality 3:* On the other hand, if you hate your job, and the prevailing "un-written" policy is to go to work in any condition, you may want to stay home and get written up, knowing you might get fired and collect unemployment.

In this scenario, depending on the consequence you choose, you will be setting a boundary that says which is more important to you at this time: your health or your career.

**Scenario 3. Your savings account vs his car payment:** Let's say you have a boyfriend who is not good at managing his money. He gets behind on his car payments. His car is going to be re-possessed. He wants you to loan him $5000 to catch up his payments, and he promises to pay you back. What are the realities and possible consequences?

*Reality 1:* Based on his poor car payment performance, he is not likely to pay you back promptly, if ever. That could mean a loss of your $5000.

*Reality 2:* You loan him the money. He gets his car back, but falls behind again and expects you to rescue him again.

Based on these possible realities, the most likely consequences to you are negative. This boyfriend has poor money management, so it's not a good risk to loan him your money, which took your time and effort to save. The possible consequences indicate it would be wise to set a boundary and let him know you're sorry he is in this situation, but he will need to find other options than borrowing your savings. You need to allow him to experience the results of his behaviors.

Do you see how looking at possible consequences can help you determine where to set your boundaries?

## You Can Use Timing to Discern Priority

Priorities are similar to boundaries. It can be helpful to consider timing to determine when you want to set your boundaries. For example:

Should I clean my house for a party, or finish my report? If the party is tonight, and the report is not due for another week, then timing says the priority should be cleaning my house.

On the other hand, if the report is due tomorrow morning, but my party is not till next weekend, my timing consideration says do the report now. Make sense?

Another way you can use timing to help set your boundaries, is to "time block" on your calendar. You start by filling in spaces on your calendar with your Center Circle items first, such as the time you want to work out each day, your weekly support group, your monthly hair appointment, and your annual physical. Don't cancel or skip any of these scheduled blocks... especially for something that is from one of the outer circles.

This principle is also shown via the often-used story of the Big Rocks.

*A professor showed his class an empty gallon jar. He then filled it with golf ball-sized rocks and asked his class if the jar was full, they said, "Yes." He then poured in some marble sized rocks, which slid into places around the larger rocks, and asked if the jar was full. Again, the students said, "Yes." Next he poured in sand, which filled in the open spaces. He again asked the question, "Is the jar full?" The students once again said, "Yes, it is full!" Finally, he added a pitcher of water, and the gallon jar was full.*

The point of this story is, if the professor puts the water, the sand, or the marble-sized rocks in first, he will not be able to add the big rocks. Remember, the big rocks represent your center circle, your self-care items, they are the most important and need to always go in first.

## Two Good Choices?

Sometimes you may have a challenge with deciding between two good options. How do you determine which is the priority?

First, since both are good options, then either one is a good choice for you. Don't stress about trying to figure out which is the perfect or "right" one. Did you know, most executive decisions are made by instinct or emotion and then justified with logic? There is no crystal ball to tell you which is the best choice, but there are a few methods you can use.

Ask the Universe or your Higher Power. Many women ask and then listen for a "still, small voice." Or you can close your eyes and think of each option. One of the options may seem light, while the other seems dark. Some women feel a sense of peace when they think of one of the options, and anxiety when they think of the other. All of these are ways you can use to receive spiritual guidance.

Another method, is to flip a coin after assigning heads to one option and tails to the other. When using this method, it isn't the flip of the coin in itself that's instructive. Instead, it is important to observe how you feel about the result. For instance, if it lands on tails and you immediately think, "Darn, I wanted heads!" this method has clarified your decision for you. I personally don't know why we can't just ask ourselves and get the same answer, but flipping the coin seems to bring our true preferences to the surface.

# Boundaries in Relationships

Many women seem to be unaware of the potential power they have in relationships. Instead, in their desire to be loved, some women become compliant and passive and even allow themselves to be treated poorly. It can be traumatizing for a woman to set boundaries, because some men are controlling and can become belligerent when challenged. Our need for a companion can be so strong, we may allow ourselves to suffer abuse rather than face the fear of being alone, or the conflict that ensues when we stand up for ourselves. And yet, to maintain a happy, healthy balance in relationships, it is absolutely necessary for both people to be authentic in setting boundaries about what is and isn't working for them.

So, ask yourself, am I allowing others to trespass over my boundaries? When we allow others to manipulate us with belligerence, guilt-making or other forms of disrespect, we are allowing them to ignore our boundaries. When we feel tense, insecure, anxious or angry, it is often a clue that our boundaries are being disregarded. It is our responsibility to speak up about our boundaries. Here are some examples of *relationship* boundaries:

## 1. You decide how you are willing to be treated.

It may be hard for you to believe you have power in your relationships. Perhaps you feel like the victim of a controlling and critical man? As long as you allow his negative behavior to continue, you *are* a victim. But you are not powerless, you have a choice in whether this continues. You may need to make the change.

Here is a true story:

## Cecelia and Carl

*A young woman named Cecelia fell in love and was married to Carl. Over time, they had two children. Carl gradually became unappreciative, and criticized her cooking, her housekeeping, and even her appearance. Initially, Cecilia tried to please him by scurrying to pick up the children's toys, find new recipes, and even change her looks.*

*Cecelia pointed out the things she was doing for him and asked him repeatedly to stop criticizing her. This caused numerous arguments in which he dismissed her feelings and discounted the validity of her complaints. Rather than appreciating her efforts, Carl's negative attitude actually got worse.*

*With coaching, Cecelia came to realize that Carl's negative attitude was unacceptable. Although she would never accept such rude behavior from her children, she was enabling (allowing) her husband to treat her with disrespect. She also realized her children were observing their poor example of marriage, and she didn't want them to absorb this negative pattern.*

*Since Carl was unwilling to change, based on his response to her repeated complaints and requests, Cecelia needed to decide how to set her boundaries... and choose the consequences needed to maintain the boundary she set. She needed to make a choice about the treatment she would allow from Carl.*

*After a great deal of thought, although it was scary for her, Cecelia told her husband that she wanted and expected a marriage in which both partners were equals and treated each other with respect, love, and kindness. She told Carl that she believed they could have that kind of marriage, but unless their marriage changed, she wanted a divorce.*

*Carl was shocked! He had been unaware of how upset she was about his negativity, because he had ignored her complaints and requests. Carl came from a family in which there was constant disrespect and criticism, which was considered normal. His treatment of Cecelia was better than what he had observed in his own family, so he thought "she has it good." Carl actually did love Cecelia and their children. He did not want a divorce.*

*When Cecelia set her boundary and told him the potential consequences, he began to change.*

*Now, if Carl complains about her cooking, Cecelia calmly says, "Honey, you don't have to eat it, if you don't like it. You are welcome to fix yourself something else." And if he gets hostile when speaking to her, she has let him know she will leave the room, until he has calmed down and is ready to speak respectfully. As for his negative comments about her appearance, she has told him he is welcome to make any positive comments about her appearance, but unsolicited negative comments are not acceptable.*

*Cecelia's boundary setting has strength because she is willing to initiate change (e.g. by leaving the room, disengaging, pointing out alternatives, or even getting a divorce) if Carl does not improve.*

*All is not yet perfect, but since setting her boundaries, Cecelia feels there has been great improvement. She can see, that, by consistent management of her boundaries, Carl's respect and loving behavior toward her will continue to grow. Cecelia is no longer willing to allow poor treatment, therefore, Carl's treatment of her has changed.*

## 2. You choose the level of trust you expect.
(More about Trust in Chapter 5)

Some men come from families or cultures in which extra-marital affairs are considered normal. Some women accept this. However, most women feel betrayed in this situation, and believe that their husband no longer loves them as much. This wedge of betrayal will need to be dealt with if the couple chooses to stay together after the infidelity.

As in the previous scenario regarding treatment, you also have the power to choose the level of trust you expect in your relationships.

Here is a true story:

## Nancy and Ned

*Nancy had been married 16 years when she discovered her husband, Ned, had been having an affair for more than a year. The other woman, Sasha, had even been to their home numerous times for social gatherings. Nancy had thought Sasha was her friend.*

*Nancy was deeply hurt by this betrayal and she was furious at both Ned and Sasha. At first, Ned suggested that maybe the three of them could maintain their friendship. Nancy said, "Are you crazy, absolutely not!"*

*Nancy considered divorce, but then she thought about all she and Ned had in common, all they had shared over the years. Although she was very angry, Nancy still loved her husband, but she had lost most of her trust in him.*

*Nancy decided she wanted to keep her marriage, but she didn't know if it was possible to rebuild the trust. When Ned was faced with the possibility of losing Nancy, he too thought of all they had built together and realized that he valued his marriage more than his affair with Sasha. He was anxious to rebuild trust with Nancy.*

*With coaching, Nancy clarified her boundaries. First, she insisted that her husband never see or contact Sasha again; no phone calls, emails or texts. He readily agreed. I asked Nancy what else Ned could do to rebuild her trust in him.*

*She wanted more of his time and attention, to be more involved in projects together. They decided to remodel their home and buy new furnishings. This joint effort and investment of money helped her feel he was more committed to their marriage. They also did more date nights and social activities together. She felt the strength of his sincere desire to rebuild trust with her.*

*Additionally, Nancy realized that she had not held herself as a full equal in their marriage. She had treated his career and his activities as though they had more value than hers. So Nancy decided she wanted to pursue a career she had dreamed of but never acted on. She wanted her own business restoring and selling antiques. She created a workshop in their basement and bought several pieces which she enjoyed refinishing and selling. Nancy's success increased her self-esteem and*

123

*impressed her husband. Now she feels more independent and equal in the marriage.*

*After several years they both feel they are happier and have a better marriage than ever.*

I know that it can be very challenging to set boundaries. You may be afraid people will get angry, or leave you, or do something vengeful. It can be scary! But, if you don't take care of yourself, and put yourself in your Center Circle, it's not reasonable to expect that anyone else will either. It's up to you to decide who and what you will allow inside your boundaries. You get to choose the kind of treatment you accept, and the level of trust you expect. Even though there may be "herds" who want to cross your fence, you get to make the choices of who and what to allow inside.

You get to choose...

## Setting Your Boundaries

When you're in a relationship, it's important to let your partner know your boundaries, and declare what will happen if he ignores them. It's always possible that he is unaware of your boundaries, like in the story of Carl and Cecelia above. As soon as you notice that your Man-imal is crossing one of your boundaries, you will need to speak up to inform him.

As a coach, one of the main things I do is help my clients to set their boundaries, and then give them encouragement to maintain their new boundary, especially when their partner is uncooperative.

It is important to set boundaries early in a relationship because it creates the pattern for future treatment. In the initial stages of dating, most men want to impress you and try to show their best behavior. So if a new man is disrespectful or belligerent early on, it is a definite Red Flag.

Studies have shown that without clear boundaries, the negative behavior will continue, usually increase, sometimes even into physical violence.

If you set healthy boundaries in the beginning, either his poor behavior will become apparent and you have the option of ending the relationship, or he will respect your boundaries and the relationship can move forward.

Stop that "elephant" before he crosses your boundary!

Since all of this makes good sense, why don't women set and/or maintain good boundaries?

- You may fear conflict, other's anger or disapproval.

- You may fear a loss of love; loneliness or abandonment.

- You may fear that you're not being kind.

- You may feel guilty about not giving.

- You may over identify with other's loss.

Perhaps, due to some of the above fears, you don't speak up when your boundaries are being ignored. Instead, you may passively comply. This creates a problem, because even though you may smile on the surface, inwardly you may begin harboring resentment. This inward resentment is a classic setup for passive-aggressive behavior, which will gradually erode any relationship. Whenever you are not authentic (true to yourself), it will create distance in your relationship. This is always true!

Now you know lots of reasons why it's important to manage your boundaries. But management can be difficult, because it requires:

o   Awareness of your own boundaries

o   Making decisions about what you really want

o   Finding the right words to clarify your position

o   The possibility of conflict with others

o   Willingness to allow other people to experience their own pain and/or consequences

## Sarah's Boundaries

Remember Sarah, who thought she had found her True Love? She was so happy and excited to end the dating game and move forward with her life. Although I thought it might be premature, after just a couple of months they had the "exclusivity talk" and decided to be monogamous. Sarah committed with her whole heart.

But Sarah's poor relationship with her father had led her to believe she should be compliant and quick to forgive. She did not stay aware her boundaries were gradually being disrespected. She made excuses for her man's bad behavior. Here are some of the Red Flags she ignored:

1. Now that he was no longer on his "best behavior" Sarah observed her man yelling at this young son, and even calling him names.

2. Although her man had a very good income and he knew she was a single mom with very limited finances, he asked her to pay for expensive things beyond her budget, such as splitting the cost of a fancy hotel room he chose.

3. She also gradually became aware that every time she brought up an issue, he would turn the conversation to be all about him and his concerns.

4. And the biggest Red Flag of all... Sarah was embarrassed and didn't share her concerns with her girlfriends. She really wanted this man to be "the one." Subconsciously, Sarah knew that if she told her girlfriends about his bad behavior, they would tell her to leave him.

5. Because Sarah thought she had found her Ideal Man (and forgot there was more work to do to build a long-term loving relationship), she had stopped coaching. In short, she cut off all her support. Now she was feeling overwhelmed and discouraged.

In the next chapter we're going to cover how to manage your feelings.

**Note for single mothers:** Regarding Circles of Responsibility, when you are a single mom and dating, your children should be in the second circle, not the third. Your first loyalty needs to be to them and finding a man who will love and care for them.

It is a Red Flag if you see a man you are dating be disrespectful and critical toward your children. After you filter out the men who are not worthy of the role of father figure, then you can choose a good man to commit to. Then, and only then, you form a parenting team with your new husband. At that point, your children move to the third circle, because children need to bond to parents who are a team, and not be a wedge between them.

I really want you to learn to be happy and have a truly satisfying love relationship! As more women learn how to do this, there will be happier families and less incidence of divorce. More children will be raised who understand healthy boundaries. As this healthy love spreads, we will have happier communities...and eventually, through the ripple effect, a happier world. That's my ultimate goal! I'd love to hear your comments and questions. Please send email to: Angeline@GorillaLove.com.

# Chapter 3

# Chapter 4:

# "Why Do I Feel This Way?"

*"Thoughts are the shadows of our feelings -
always darker, emptier and simpler."*

— Friedrich Nietzsche

Chapter 4

# What Are Feelings, Anyway?

Sometimes you may feel overwhelmed by your feelings, such as:

"He makes me so mad!"

"I feel so sad; I can't seem to stop crying."

"My mother drives me frickin' crazy!"

"I've heard rumors of layoffs, and it's making me so anxious I can't sleep!"

"Sometimes I'm unbelievably happy!"

If you are like most of us, you wish that you could be happy and peaceful all the time. You want life to roll along smoothly.

You may wish there were no conflicts or challenges. Unfortunately, the human experience includes lots of challenges. Nevertheless, that doesn't mean you can't feel confident and happy most of the time. I can assure you that it's possible, because I am peaceful and happy most of the time.

How is that possible?

I'm going to share the "secret" with you! One of the important skills in happy relationships is learning to be in charge of your feelings, rather than being run around by your feelings. I will also share some clues for understanding your man and his feelings. Let's start by learning about feelings: What are they, anyway? Where do feelings come from? To explain, I'm going to use the analogy of a fire.

    ○    Feelings may seem like smoke.

    ○    They float around in the air.

    ○    You can't control them.

    ○    They can make you cry.

    ○    They make it hard for you to see clearly.

FUEL: To build a fire, you start with the fuel. In this analogy, the fuel is our attitudes and beliefs.

MATCH: Next you need something to start the fire, like a match. We call this the "trigger event." It could be the driver who cuts in front of you. Maybe your Man-imal didn't call when he said he would. Perhaps your sister critiques your housekeeping. Or, the sales clerk was rude.

SMOKE: Finally comes the smoke. The kind of smoke you get, will depend on the fuel you used. Fragrant fuel makes lovely smoke, like incense. Stinky fuel makes toxic smoke. And toxic smoke can kill.

Most people try to change their feelings by trying to change the trigger event. This usually means trying to change other people's behavior: the driver who cut you off, the rude clerk, or your sister. However, we usually have very little control over others. Actually, the real key is to change the fuel... your underlying attitudes and beliefs.

- o Stinky attitudes create stinky feelings; in the same way that expectations or perfectionism creates criticism.

- o Toxic beliefs create toxic feelings; in the way racial bias can create hate.

- o Lovely attitudes create lovely feelings; such as positive assumptions about others' intentions.

Here is a story, which was shared by Stephen Covey, to demonstrate how feelings work.

## On The Subway

*Late one afternoon, in New York, a man and his three children boarded the subway. The man sat down, put his elbows on his knees, his head in his hands, and closed his eyes. His children began to run "wild." As they laughed and chased each other, they bumped into the other passengers and stepped on people's feet. Their father ignored all of it. The other passengers began to get annoyed. They believed the father should be responsible and control his children. Some passengers began to mumble under their breath.*

*Eventually, one woman angrily spoke up, "Sir, will you please do something about your children!" Everyone watched to see how the man would react.*

*The man's eyes popped opened and his head jerked up. He looked around and said, "Oh, I'm so sorry! I wasn't paying attention. We just left the hospital where my wife, their mother, passed away. They are probably reacting to that." Then he called his children to come sit quietly beside him.*

*At his words, some of the other passengers gasped. Their anger and frustration immediately drained away. Their faces softened. Some said, "I'm so sorry for your loss." One woman offered the children some cookies from her bag of groceries.*

This story is a good illustration of the way feelings work and how they can change. Our feelings, like a fire, start with the *fuel* of our attitudes and beliefs. In this example, many of the passengers held the belief that fathers should not allow their children to bother or inconvenience the other passengers.

Next comes the match or the *triggering event*. In this case, it was the rowdy children, while the father appeared to simply ignore their behavior.

Finally come the *feelings*. Because of their beliefs, the passengers initially felt angry. But their feelings changed when they got new information...the "back story" of the family's situation, and what had occurred that day.

Your attitudes and beliefs can be changed through gathering information (a back story), and this will change your feelings. When you see things from a different view, it is called a paradigm shift.

If this is the first time you have heard this concept about where feelings come from, it may initially be hard to understand. You may want to say, "Well, anyone would have been angry on that subway." And it's certainly true that many people would have reacted with anger.

But, there really are many other possible feelings or reactions, depending on the under-lying beliefs. For example, if you believed that all children should be allowed to run and play, even if they bumped into people or stepped on their toes, then you would have reacted with different feelings.

Here is another way of explaining feelings, as described by Dr. Wayne Dyer, from his blog on August 29, 2015:

*I was preparing to speak at an I Can Do It conference and I decided to bring an orange on stage with me as a prop for my lecture. I opened a conversation with a bright young fellow of about twelve who was sitting in the front row.*

*"If I were to squeeze this orange as hard as I could, what would come out?" I asked him.*

*He looked at me like I was a little crazy and said, "Juice, of course."*

*"Do you think apple juice could come out of it?" "No!" he laughed.*

*"What about grapefruit juice?" "No!"*

*"What would come out of the orange?" "Orange juice, of course."*

*"Why? Why when you squeeze an orange does orange juice come out?"*

*He may have been getting a little exasperated with me at this point.*

*"Well, it's an orange and that's what's inside."*

*I nodded. "Let's assume that this orange isn't an orange, but it's you. And someone squeezes you, puts pressure on you, says something you don't like, and offends you. And out of you comes anger, hatred, bitterness, fear. Why? The answer, as our young friend has told us, is because that's what's inside."*

It's one of the great lessons of life. What comes out when life squeezes you? When someone hurts or offends you? If anger, pain and fear come out of you, it's because that's what's inside. It doesn't matter who does the squeezing—your mother, your brother, your children, your boss, the government. If someone says something about you that you don't like, what comes out of you is what's inside. And what's inside is up to you, that's your choice.

When someone puts the pressure on you, and out of you comes anything other than love, it's because that's what you've allowed to be inside. Once you take away all those negative things you don't want in your life and replace them with love, you'll find yourself living a highly functioning life.

So, now you know that feelings come from the attitudes and beliefs that are inside us. But, where did those come from?

## We Learned from Our Families

We learn our family's attitudes and beliefs. We learn their expectations. We learn what our family believes is right and wrong. We learn our family's language for handling feelings. We learn their ways of dealing with disagreements.

As you find insights to your inner attitudes and beliefs, you will probably find some that you no longer want to keep. Be sure to forgive yourself for any undesirable attitudes and beliefs you inherited from your family, such as racism or bigotry. As a child, you had no control over what you were taught or learned from examples set by the adults who raised you. Now you can choose for yourself what you want to believe.

You can educate yourself about any issue which you find generates strong feelings in you. Find out more about that issue. As you learn, you will develop understanding—even if you don't agree. Your understanding will help reduce your stress and allow a more loving attitude.

Here is an example:

I have had the opportunity to learn about meditation through a study of Tibetan Buddhism. This created a love in my heart for the Tibetans. But, then I felt angry toward the Chinese for invading their country, killing many of the monks, and destroying temples.

Later I became friends with a Chinese man who was visiting America while teaching math at a local private school. One day I asked him, "How do you feel about the invasion of Tibet?" Since he is a well-educated man, I fully expected him to be critical about it. But, he sincerely said to me, "It has really helped the Tibetan people. We have built lots of infrastructure for them, including schools and hospitals. It was a very backward country before."

At first I was shocked. I couldn't believe that he thought those things justified the destruction of the Tibetan culture. And, although I still don't share his perspective, I can now understand his view. And, it gave me further insight into how the Dalai Lama, who is in exile for his own safety, can refer to the Chinese as, "my friends, the enemy."

Can you think of some of your attitudes or beliefs that are causing stress in your life? Maybe an area of conflict between you and a friend or family member? Perhaps if you get curious about why they see things the way they do, you may be able to build a bridge of understanding, even if you continue to disagree.

## Get Curious not Critical

When we get curious instead of critical, it can help us change our feelings. Here is another fictional story to explain this concept.

## The Easter Ham

*A young couple, John and Judy, had been married only a few years. It was Easter time, and Judy's family was coming for dinner. She wanted to serve ham, based on her family's traditional recipe. But, when she suggested this to her husband John, he responded with frustration, "I don't like the way you cook ham, you always waste some of it." Judy felt hurt, and said, "I just cook it the same way my mother always did." John wasn't happy, but he agreed they could have the ham for Easter dinner.*

*On Easter Sunday, with the extended family gathered in their home, John found a quiet moment with his mother-in-law in the kitchen and gently asked her about the family way of preparing ham. He said, "Why do you cut off both ends of the ham, before you add the glaze and put it in the oven?"*

*"Oh," she laughed, "it's because the only pan I have is too small for the ham." John laughed, too. With his new knowledge of the back story, John knew how he could help Judy "update" the family recipe and cook the whole ham. He was no longer frustrated with her.*

So, who is responsible for how you feel? You are! If you want to change your feelings from something negative, you can get curious and gather information (like John above), or you can create a back story.

## Creating a Back Story

My second daughter, Jillena, is a mom with two young children. She spends a lot of time in her car, in the role of chauffeur, driving her kids to activities. It used to really frustrate her when someone would rush ahead of her or cut her off in traffic. But, now she invents a back story for these drivers. She tells herself, "He's in a hurry to the hospital, because his wife is in labor and the baby is coming." Jillena says aloud, "I hope he makes it in time!"

Even though Jillena knows she has created this back story, it changes her attitude and reduces her stress.

Actually, it's not usually someone's behavior that upsets us, instead it's usually our assumptions about their behavior, based on our attitudes and beliefs. For your own sense of inner peace and happiness, it's best to assume a positive intention. If the other person is a stranger, you can make up a back story for him. But, if you are in a relationship, you can get curious and ask yourself (or him):

What made him act like that?

What is he trying to achieve?

Why is he feeling that way?

What is he really trying to say?

And, why did I react the way I did?

This is one of the biggest "secrets" to understanding your man's behavior and feelings. These questions shift us away from criticism or judgment. It helps us avoid any triggers toward negativity which we may unconsciously have.

If you ask your man, from a place of genuine curiosity, with a caring heart, you will gain some new insights and understanding. It is important to create an emotionally safe environment by avoiding criticism. When you create a safe environment for your man to share his thoughts, feelings and motivations with you, it will increase feelings of connection and intimacy in your relationship.

As you become skilled at managing your own feelings and understanding those of your man, it is important to understand the difference between empathy and sympathy.

# Empathy Vs Sympathy

Empathy is feeling what others feel. We feel empathy when we understand. Empathy brings us together.

Sympathy is feeling pity. Sympathy separates us.

To watch a really cute video by Brene' Brown about the difference between empathy and sympathy, go to this link:

https://www.youtube.com/watch?v=1Evwgu369Jw

But there are limits to empathy. You may understand how he feels and even why he behaves the way he does, but that is no excuse to allow physical or emotional abuse, or repeated dishonesty.

Forgiveness doesn't mean putting up with continuous bad behavior. Remember, you are responsible to determine the treatment you will allow. So set your boundaries. Take good care of yourself!

# Sarah Decides to Communicate

In the previous chapter, regarding boundaries, do you remember Sarah was realizing ways in which her boundaries were being ignored? Sarah really wanted to be done with dating! She had tied all her hopes on this man being her Ideal Man. But, now she was feeling overwhelmed and discouraged. Before Sarah learned how to handle her own feelings, she often felt upset or worried, especially if she thought her man was angry with her.

Her anxiety would cause her to abandon her own best interests in a desire to placate him. Worse, she didn't understand why he acted the ways he did. Why did he get angry over things that seemed so unimportant?

Now, she realized that her upset feelings were a clue for her to check within herself and ask herself, "why do I feel this way?"

When Sarah allowed herself to be objective and really look at her relationship, she realized there was a lot she wasn't happy with. In fact, she was losing trust in this man—quickly, and for good reason. She decided she would need to communicate with him about the things that were bothering her, rather than let them slide in hopes the issues would resolve by themselves.

In the next chapter on communications, I will share some examples of negative and positive ways of handling disagreements. Learning communication skills will be a key for you in building a healthy relationship.

It is my goal to help you create a safe and loving environment where you and your man can be authentic and openly share your thoughts and feelings. If you have questions or comments, please send me an email: Angeline@GorillaLove.com. I look forward to hearing from you!

# Chapter 4

# Chapter 5:

# "I Think I Have a Communication Problem!"

*"Take advantage of every opportunity to practice your communication skills so that when important occasions arise, you will have the gift, the style, the sharpness, the clarity, and the emotions to affect other people."*

— Jim Rohn

Other than the first chapter, which included the profiles of each of our 12 Man-imals, this is the largest chapter in the book. Learning to communicate your thoughts and feelings with authenticity is like learning a foreign language. It will require learning several basic principles and *lots* of practice. Please don't be discouraged! I've had three years of French and still struggle to learn a language I love. In fact, one of my bucket-list dreams is to live in France for six months to a year, so that I can become fluent. So, be patient with yourself about learning this *new language*!

## What Is Good Communication?

We all know how to talk, right? So why is communication so difficult?

I know I keep "blaming" everything on our families, but that is where most of us learned about relationships, and certainly about communicating. Often, some really bad habits are passed down in families, until someone struggles enough to change them.

Unfortunately, most of us learned some communication styles that sabotage our desire to build a loving relationship. It's not your fault you learned these negative patterns or beliefs, you may even fully believe you have learned to think and feel differently. But your familial patterns may be engrained to the point you no longer notice their negative impact.

Now, you have the opportunity to learn some new ways that will enhance your love life! Even the negative patterns you discover you are carrying, can be changed with deliberate intention and action.

This may be a surprise, but good communication isn't about talking! It's about understanding each other. If you're not understanding each other, you're not really communicating.

You're just talking *at* each other.

Real understanding takes skill, because people don't always say what they mean. Behind their words are their true feelings, but they may feel too vulnerable to say them. It requires your full attention to gather the clues to what they're "trying" to say. You need to be a detective.

This is especially true when you try to understand your man, because he has more than likely been taught it's not masculine to share his feelings. That masculine belief is pervasive in Western culture.

To be an ideal detective is to be curious, with an open heart and mind, and to avoid pre-judgement. You need to watch his facial expression, his body language, and of course listen to his words. Being a really good listener, with your eyes, ears, and heart, is the biggest part of being a good communicator.

But most of us don't really listen when the other person is speaking. Instead, we are busily forming our response. We are planning our defense. We are not curious about how he feels. We may even be making critical assumptions about what we imagine he thinks and feels.

## Reasons People Hide Their Feelings

While you are learning to be a detective, trying to figure out what your man thinks and feels, let me share some of the reasons why people hide their emotions. Most of these reasons were learned at home, in a family that was not comfortable with sharing thoughts and feelings. Some of these reasons may also apply to you.

○ His parents were critical and/or controlling, and got angry with him, especially if he disagreed with them.

○ He may think that any "discussion" involves getting into a fight. And he wants to avoid conflict with you.

○ He may lack good communication skills and doesn't know what to say.

○ Perhaps he thinks his preferences are unimportant.

○ He may think the only way to "get his way" is to be a bully, and now he wants to avoid that.

All of these may also be reasons why he (and you) have avoided being open about thoughts and feelings. Look at your own behavior, and the feelings that come up when you try to express the way you feel, with your man, or with a friend. Where do you suppose your reactions came from? How does your man see these behaviors?

## Reasons to AVOID Communicating

I'm going to share some skills regarding good communication. But first, there are actually some reasons you should *avoid* starting a conversation with your man, at least for the moment. Before you start a conversation, ask yourself if you have a hidden agenda, such as...

- To make your man feel bad, stupid, or guilty

- To unload your anger, tension, or stress

- To show you're hurt, by hurting him

- To make yourself be seen as right

- To alienate him and make him feel alone

- To dominate or control him

- To pass the buck and make him responsible

- To blame him, so you don't feel wrong

- To hide your real feelings, hurt, pain, or fear

- To hide your failures

If one or more of these is the real reason you want to have a talk with him, the conversation will not go well. These hidden agendas will make him feel defensive. They are all win/lose strategies. They are not focused on solution or win/win. So, before you start the conversation, take some time to check in with yourself. Let go of the temptation to "hit" him with your message. Later in this chapter I will give you a tool to use to handle conflict in a more productive way.

## Negative Fighting Styles

In some families, when there is a disagreement, it's not a discussion—approached with respect, with a desire to clarify the issues and to understand each other—instead it's a battle! A win-lose fighting style automatically means that someone must lose, so that the other person can win. All of the following tactics are strategies that attempt to create a winner and a loser.

*Character Assassination*...when using this tactic, one opponent is drawing attention away from the issue, and instead wants to discredit the other person. A really ugly example is the way some defense attorneys will try to protect their client from a rape charge by painting a picture of the woman as having loose morals. Some families use this same strategy, to discredit each other.

*Name Calling or Sarcasm*.... this is used to belittle a person, to discount them. It is not about the issue, instead it's used to weaken the other person or reduce their credibility. For example, saying sarcastically," Oh yeah, we know how smart you are!"

Some families think it's okay to use sarcasm, because they assume everyone does, and therefore it doesn't really mean anything. Here's the problem: To be able to live with negative sarcasm and not react to its sting, family members have to put on emotional armor, which creates a barrier between them. This distance making is not ideal!

Maybe in your dysfunctional family-of-origin, it was necessary to protect yourself with emotional armor. In an ideal loving relationship, you want to create a safe environment where partners can be open and vulnerable with one another. To create a safe environment, in a loving relationship, the couple needs to agree to stop using negative sarcasm. It is part of setting healthy boundaries.

*Giving False Information*...saying anything to distract from the issue, including telling lies to stack the deck. When dishonesty is used, one of the challenges is you will feel the need to defend against the lying. If you accuse your partner of lying, it may become a battle of accusation and defense... "he said – she said" ... and is no longer about the issue.

*Keeping Score*...if you're focused on winning, naturally, you're going to keep score. If it feels you're losing more than winning, you may find yourself resorting to some of the negative tactics listed above.

Perhaps you have used some of these negative strategies in the past, now you're learning that all these strategies destroy, rather than build relationships. These negative tactics do not resolve issues, therefore there is always residual resentment, and the distance grows. If you find that you or your man are using negative fighting styles, you need to create an opportunity (not in the heat of battle) to discuss them and how they function to create distance and distrust.

## Create A Safe Environment

Next, I want to share some things you can do to create a "safe" environment for both of you to be open and vulnerable when sharing your true feelings. In a family that has healthy boundaries, it's usually fairly easy to find a peaceful way to settle disagreements.

But most women need some help with learning to handle challenging conversations. Before you sit down for a serious conversation, get his agreement to set a "structure" for communication where you can BOTH feel comfortable to share. Here are some BASIC guidelines:

- o Choose a quiet time and place, not public.

- o No yelling (it is scary).

- o No sarcasm (it is discounting).

- o No swearing (it is disrespectful).

- o No violence or threats of violence (it is bullying).

o No threats to leave the relationship (it is a manipulation).

o Either one can ask for a postponement if feeling overwhelmed, but set a specific time to meet again.

Because you are both new to this process, it will probably be uncomfortable the first few times. Communication involves working with feelings, and feelings are scary for a lot of people.

Either of you may break one or more of the guidelines and need to be gently reminded to stick to the process. But, gradually, with practice, as with any skill development, you will get better and better at good communication. It will become more natural and easier to stay with the process. But, most important, over time you will understand each other better.

## Good Communication Skills

After you have set a structure for a safe environment and had a few conversations, you are ready for a more complete understanding of good communication skills.

There is a LOT of information here, so don't expect yourself to remember it with just one reading. You may even want to make a copy so that you can refer to it when needed. It is helpful to get his agreement to follow these as Ground Rules in your relationship:

1. Get clear about what you are trying to accomplish with this conversation. It may help to write down your goal; perhaps to resolve an issue, create greater understanding or more openness.

2. Start with a positive statement. Let your man know there's something in it for him. There's a way he will benefit. It could be any of the following: better understanding, more openness, resolution of an issue, or even improved sex, etc.

3. One person speaks at a time. Deal with one issue at a time. Both stay focused on that one issue until both feel resolved, creating a win/win.

4. As Stephen Covey taught, it's best to "seek to understand before being understood," so it's helpful to offer to listen to his perspective first. It might be wise to say something like this, "We have a difference of opinion about _____, and I am sure you have a good reason for your perspective. I would like to understand your view on this ONE issue." Do not bring up unrelated issues.

5.  Listen, really listen, with an open mind and heart. Keep asking gentle questions until you feel confident you understand his view on this one issue. For verification, reflect your new understanding of his perception back to him. Keep trying until he agrees that you understand him. (Remember that just because you understand, it doesn't automatically mean that you agree.)

6.  Work together to find a resolution that satisfies both of you: win/win. A compromise usually means one person wins and the other loses, so find a resolution that BOTH of you are comfortable with. You may not get *exactly* what you each want, but it needs to be enough that you are both satisfied and feel it's fair. Otherwise you may hold resentment.

7.  Next, it is your turn to have him listen to ONE issue from you. It is fair to take turns on one issue at a time, so that there is balance in the relationship. Ask him to hear your perspective. Remember that learning each other's back story is an opportunity to change attitudes and beliefs!

8.  Talk about yourself and your own feelings and perspectives. Do not presume to speak for the other person's thoughts and feelings. Let them tell their own.

9.  Observe your emotions; manage your voice tones. Our voice tones are actually "heard" louder than the words we use. That's why it's so important not to yell. Your voice tones need to reflect an open, caring attitude.

10. Don't use distancing language. The words we use can make others feel defensive. Avoid using controlling phrases like: you should, you have to, or you must. It also creates distance when you use global terms that are not personal, such as: anyone would, we all feel, everyone thinks, etc. Instead, it is best to speak for yourself, from your heart: I will, I feel, or I think.

11. Don't blame the other person for your feelings by saying things such as, "You make me angry!" We don't have the power to MAKE someone feel something. Feelings are the result of our own attitudes and beliefs.

12. Before saying anything, always ask yourself: Is it true? Is it kind? Is it necessary? Your words have a lot of power, and you can't take them back, once said.

13. Tell the truth and be diplomatic about it. I personally believe all "little white lies or exaggerations" should be avoided. You can build trust through a policy of honesty.

14. Give yourself a time-out if you need to calm down. If you (or he) gets overwhelmed with emotions, it's okay to postpone the meeting to another specific day and time. It is not okay to eternally postpone.

15. Keep your goal in mind; remember that you want to find resolution, build connection, and create a win-win result. It is not settled until both people are satisfied. When the goal is to understand each other, and find resolution, rather than to win, then respect and kindness become a basic part of the process.

16. In a relationship, if one person loses, then the relationship is diminished. To strengthen the relationship, both people need to feel that they have benefited from the discussion.

17. Sometimes it may be hard for one person to understand the perspective of the other. In times like this it may be helpful to literally change places. Switch the chairs you are sitting in and pretend you are the other person, then speak from their perspective to explain their position. Then ask if you got it right.

18. And of course, no name calling, no sarcasm, and no violence or threats of violence.

Practice the above skills as often as possible with everyone around you, so that they become familiar and easy for you to use.

# The DESC Message

Here is another communication skill you can use to handle conflicts or disagreements. It's called a DESC message. I don't know who developed it, but my mother, psychologist Dr. Lorraine Manderscheid, taught it to me.

**D = Describe the situation non-blamefully.** Learning this skill can be challenging initially, because you are focused on what he did wrong....so how do you say it without blame? Here's a hint: remove any "YOU" messages and replace them with "I" messages instead. For example: instead of saying, "You are always late!" Say, "I want to be on time."

**E = Express your feelings.** Keep your statement about your feelings as simple as possible, for example: "I feel frustrated," or "I feel angry," or "I don't feel respected."

**S = Specify the change you want.** Again, keep this simple, and very specific. For example: "I want you to be on time for our dates," not, "I want you to respect me."

**C = Consequences, positive.** Tell him what the positive result can be. For example: "Being on time will reduce my stress and tension, instead of us having to rush to get to our dinner reservations. It will allow me to look forward to our dates."

*Then wait* to see how he responds. Hopefully he will agree and commit to making a change.

But, if he doesn't...

**C = Consequences, negative.** Give the negative consequences, if he doesn't want to co-operate. For example: "If agreeing to be on time does not work for you, please know that I want to be on time, so I will leave at the appropriate time, even if you are not here."

One thing this process does is bring the issue to a head. It becomes very clear whether or not he is willing to make the changes you have requested.

## Suzie Used The DESC Method

One of my clients, Suzie, used this process when dealing with her bookkeeper. He was consistently late with his reports, and the reports often had errors. She was very frustrated with him and had asked him nicely, repeatedly, to do better, but he just made excuses.

During our coaching, Suzie acknowledged that she was the employer and therefore he needed to fulfill her expectations to her satisfaction. She needed to set a boundary. This was scary for her, because she usually avoided standing up for herself. However, with my encouragement, she decided to use the DESC message to set a boundary about her expectations.

Suzie wrote out the DESC steps and emailed them to him. He responded with defensiveness and criticism of her...and he quit! At first Suzie was upset. She didn't think this process worked! But, I pointed out to her that this unsatisfactory man, who had been a problem for some time, was now no longer a thorn in her side. She was free to get a new bookkeeper.

This is one of the *positive* things that happens when we use good communication skills and set boundaries. Toxic people will move away from us. They often kick and scream and try to blame us for their bad behavior. But, they don't want to hang around, when we hold them accountable. Gradually your world will become more peaceful. You will be happier!

# The Five Love Languages

If you haven't already, I recommend you get a copy of *The Five Love Languages* by Gary D. Chapman. It contains a very simple but elegant take on communicating love. Basically, he explains that people often misread each other's messages about love, because they speak different love languages.

**The Five Love Languages are as follows:**

1. Giving and receiving Gifts

2. Quality Time

3. Acts of Service

4. Physical Touch

5. Words of Affirmation

Dr. Chapman says that most people like to give and receive love within the same language. For example, if your Love Language is Gifts, then you probably get all excited about receiving a package and unwrapping it. You probably get similarly excited about finding the perfect gift to give to someone, then wrapping it beautifully and looking forward to seeing them unwrap it.

## Mom & Dad

Here is a story to give you an example of how miscommunication happens concerning love languages.

*My Mom's love language is Words. And my Dad's is Acts of Service. My Mom was always hoping my Dad would tell her sweet loving words. But my Dad thinks "talk is cheap." The extent of his sweet words was to say, "Where's Ma' Honey?" when he entered home every night.*

*When she gave him a greeting card that said pretty things, he wished she would have baked him a pie instead. He wanted actions, not words.*

*On the other hand, he usually pitched in to help around the house. They raised six kids, so there was always a lot to do. He usually fixed breakfast in the mornings and in the evenings he might throw in a load of laundry, start dinner, or pick up a broom and sweep the floor. Do you think Mom "received" the love?*

*Unfortunately, no. Instead, she thought he was unhappy with her homemaking skills. A total mismatch of languages!*

This was a total misunderstanding simply because they did not know how to read each other's love languages.

# Chapter 5

## **Our First Christmas**

Here is another story for you.

*My love language is Gifts. My husband, Dixon's love language is Words. (He and my Mom got along great!) But I didn't know about the love languages concept when we shared our first Christmas, more than twenty years ago. I bought him a big, comfy robe with a pair of matching slippers, several CDs, a couple of shirts, and a sweater. It was a lot of presents because I wanted him to know I really loved him!*

*On Christmas morning I was so excited and looked forward to seeing his happy face as he opened all his presents. And I could barely wait to see what he got for me! But, as he opened present after present, he didn't look happy. In fact, he gradually looked less and less happy. But, I wasn't really paying attention because I couldn't wait to open my presents. We hadn't put them under a tree, so I didn't have any idea how many he had bought, or how big they were.*

*When Dixon finished opening his gifts, I said, "Oh honey, I'm ready for my presents! I can't wait to see what you got me!"*

*He handed me an envelope. In it was a letter, and a small antique cross on a black silk string. First I read the two-page letter. It was thoughtful and sort of poetic. The letter explained he'd had the cross for many years and it had sentimental value to him, but now he wanted me to have it.*

*"Okay," I thought, "that's kinda sweet." And I said, "That's nice, what else?"*

*He said, "What do you mean, what else?"*

*I replied, "Well this letter is nice, but what presents did you get for me?"*

*He said, "That is the present. It's the nicest letter I've ever written. I've worked on it for days."*

*I was dumbfounded. I couldn't decide whether to cry or get angry. Was he just cheap? I said, "But a letter is not a present. I bought you presents."*

*He looked very frustrated and said, "Yeah, you just bought stuff. My gift is personal; it has more meaning than overspending on stuff."*

Whoa boy! We had some work to do! Because my love language is *gifts* and his is *words*, we had totally misunderstood each other. We needed to learn to communicate on a whole new level!

# Parent – Adult - Child

Here is another way of increasing your communication skills. It's my take on a form of psychoanalytic therapy, called Transactional Analysis, which was developed by Eric Berne, and was popular in the 60s. This is not true to *his* process; it is my own version.

Here is the concept:

There are three different psychological aspects to every person.

1. The Critical Parent: This is an accumulation of all the negative messages you absorbed while growing up. Every time one of your parents, or a teacher, or any other authority figure, gave you a message that you weren't "okay," it got stored in your brain. All their messages about how you *should* be, every failure they pointed out to you, every criticism is recorded. Now those negative messages repeat in your head on auto-replay.

2. The Emotional Child: Your inner Child is all about emotions, happy or sad, her feelings can instantly change. And these feelings won't seem logical. Just like a 3-year-old child, your Emotional Child is impatient and impulsive. It is self-centered and into short

term, immediate gratification. Your playful side is also located in your Child. Fears and insecurities are also part of your Emotional Child.

3. The Adult: Your adult is reasonable and responsible. It plays the role of mediator between your Critical Parent and Emotional Child. The Adult listens to the Child's fears and desires. It also listens to the Parent's complaints and worries. Then the Adult reassures the Child by saying, "I will take care of you. I will see that your needs are met. I want you to be happy." And the Adult tells the Parent, "I hear your worries that the Child is being irresponsible, and I will help the Child behave wisely." The Adult is ultimately responsible for your overall, long-term happiness. Ideally you make choices from your Adult.

Every person has a different mix of these three aspects in their psychological makeup. You have these three and your man also has these three. If you graphed them, it might look like this:

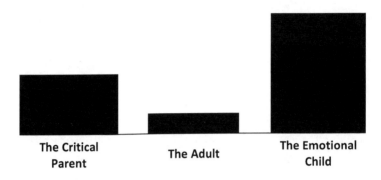

| **The Critical Parent** | **The Adult** | **The Emotional Child** |

We shift internally from one aspect to another in different situations. For example, if he starts criticizing you from his Parent, you might automatically go into your Emotional Child and feel sad and insecure. Or, when he is being irresponsible, you may go into your Parent and find yourself chastising him. But relating to someone from your Parent, usually makes the other person defensive, so it's usually better to speak from your Adult.

You want to be in your Adult as much as possible when you relate with your man. If you find you are dealing with a man who is mostly in his Child, (like the graph above), be patient and reassuring, use gentle and calm tones, while you explain the need for him to behave responsibly. On the other hand, if he is being judgmental to you and talking at you from his Parent, then stay in your Adult while you respond with boundary setting about how he treats you.

Ideally, as you were growing up, your Adult gradually became the strongest of your three aspects. Your Emotional Child needs to trust your Adult to take care of her, and to protect her from the constant negative messages of your Critical Parent.

Learning to care for yourself from your Adult is one way of managing your feelings. It is your Adult who can use the skills of boundary setting and building trust. The more you operate from your Adult, the more you will feel empowered and confident.

Here's how an ideal P-A-C graph would look:

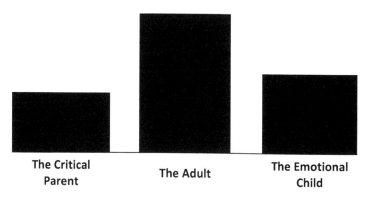

| The Critical Parent | The Adult | The Emotional Child |

## Sarah Tries Communicating

This concept (Parent-Adult-Child) was particularly helpful to Sarah. She quickly understood that her Adult could reject the constant negativity from the Critical Parent (her father's voice) within her head. She also knew that it was up to her to manage the boundaries necessary to care for her inner Child.

Sarah decided to communicate with her man about the things that were bothering her. Because she can easily become scared and "forget" to discuss the issues that really bother her, she spent a great deal of time making notes about the things she wanted to cover. Sarah wanted to be sure she spoke from her Adult.

She wanted to create a safe environment, so she asked him to set a private time when they wouldn't be disturbed, so they could talk. She set the stage by letting him know the purpose of the talk was to improve their relationship. She did not want him to mistakenly think she was breaking up with him.

When he arrived the next night for the talk, they sat down in the living room. Sarah had her notes and she started reading to him some of the guidelines for a safe environment, such as; one person speaks at a time, no name calling or sarcasm, etc.

But, instead of listening, her man got angry. He began shouting and even calling her names. He threatened to break up with her and threw her house key on the table. This was bizarre! She had pictured a nice conversation which would improve their understanding. Instead, he started giving her ultimatums. Sarah panicked and caved-in to his demands, while asking him to stay. He did, but spent another hour berating her, while she remained silent and emotionally paralyzed.

When he finally left, Sarah was devastated! She felt her heart was breaking. She cried all night, the next morning she called her girlfriends, and then she called me. Sarah was ready to be open about what wasn't working in this relationship. She wanted help and support. Sarah needed to talk with people who loved her, would listen and wouldn't be critical.

I've shared Sarah's painful experience with you, so that you will have realistic expectations about how relationships develop. Even with Sarah's excellent intentions and good preparation, it did not go well. Although this was very panful for her, she now has her eyes fully open, has quit hiding in an illusion of love, and sees the real challenges of this man.

## Your Relationship Goal

At the heart of every good relationship is feeling seen, known, and accepted as you are. This is true whether it is a romantic relationship or with your girlfriends. One way to "measure" the quality of your relationship is to ask: "How authentic are we being with each other?"

If you feel the need to hide your thoughts and feelings, or to walk on eggshells so the other person won't react negatively.... then you have work to do.

In an excellent relationship it feels safe for both people to share their thoughts and feelings. In fact, over time, you will probably come to love each other for your differences. You will laugh together over your challenges.

In closing this chapter on communications, I thought you might enjoy something more about authenticity:

## Are you a Lamborghini or a Prius?

What's your style? As you know, every guy is going to *look* when a Lamborghini drives by. But not every guy *wants* a Lamborghini. Even if he had the money, some guys are going to say "No, you know, it's high maintenance, it has no room to carry my camping gear, and the gas mileage is terrible."

Given a choice, some guys really want a Jeep…. or an SUV…. or a gas efficient Prius. But not every guy is going to *look* when a Prius drives by. So, should the little gas efficient Prius try to change itself to resemble a Lamborghini, so that all the guys will *look*? No, because then it would lose the appreciation of the guys who really *want* a Prius.

I'm sure you can guess where I'm headed with this analogy. Yes, most every guy is going to look when a Playboy Barbie walks by. But some guys are also going to say to themselves, "No, she's too high maintenance, she wouldn't want to go camping, and I'll bet her personality is terrible."

So, should you try to change yourself to resemble a Playboy Barbie, just so more guys will *look*? No, because then you will lose the appreciation of the guys who *want* your type…. the girl next door, or the earth-mother, or the tomboy, etc.

The major problem with pretending to be something you're not, is that it's not real. After a few months, or even years, he's going to say, "You're not who I thought you were." True love is based on open, intimate, authenticity. Your relationship can deepen over the years as you learn to further understand and accept each other. Obviously this kind of love cannot be built on a false foundation!

So, whatever type you are, be authentic! Shine in your own shoes.... whether they are tennis shoes, flip flops or hiking boots. Of course, that doesn't mean you shouldn't keep in shape, dress well, and learn to speak good grammar. Even a Prius gets a wash and wax on a regular basis. Just sayin!

I've given you a *ton* of information in this chapter on communications. Please don't expect yourself to master it quickly! If you are like most of us, it will take you years of practice. It's like learning any skill. You will trip and fall and skin your knees. Just get up and try again. The good news is that every time you communicate a little bit better, it will improve your life a little bit better, too. As Maya Angelou famously said, "When we know better, we do better."

The more comfortable you get using these skills, the more comfortable you will also be with being authentic. Being able to be your real self and communicate your true thoughts and feelings is *so* empowering! It will build your self-esteem and let your soul shine to the world—how attractive is that! Emotionally healthy men are attracted to women who are comfortable with themselves. It is such juicy and delicious energy. And that is a great segue to our next chapter!

For more information, you can go to my website: GorillaLove.com. I love to hear comments and suggestions from my readers! And if you would like me to personally coach you, please send an email to Angeline@GorillaLove.com.

# Chapter 5

# Chapter 6:

# "I Don't Think I Can Ever Trust a Man Again!"

*"Trust is the glue of life. It's the most essential ingredient in effective communication. It's the foundational principle that holds all relationships."*

—Stephen Covey

# Who Should You Trust, and When?

Trust is the foundation for all good relationships. But, if you have been betrayed, maybe more than once—and especially during your formative years—it may be hard for you to feel like trusting anyone. So, who should you trust? And when? Some people think...

... you shouldn't trust anyone until it's earned.

... being trusting is being naïve or foolish.

... a person is either trustworthy or not.

... trust can be demanded.

... once trust is earned, it will stay constant.

Actually, we trust different people in different ways at different times, for different things, and to different extents. For example, you may trust your banker to give you financial advice, but not to tell you how to fix your car. Or maybe you trust your BFF to tell you the truth about how your new dress looks, but not to give you financial advice. Perhaps you trust your boyfriend to fix your car, but not to give you advice on clothing styles.

In the above examples it is fairly easy to understand why you would or wouldn't give trust, because it's based on your knowledge of their areas of expertise. But sometimes we give trust based on our *feelings*.

For example, although you may trust your boyfriend to fix your car, you may not *feel* safe when he drives. If you ask him to slow down, and he dismisses your feelings with a statement like, "Don't worry, I never get in accidents," you not only don't trust his driving, but now you also don't trust him to be considerate of your feelings!

It is important to understand the different components of trust because trust is so key in relationships. I'm going to give you concepts to enable you to measure the trustworthiness of people in your life. This will help you determine who and when it is safe to trust. Giving your trust to a man is a precious gift, so don't give it too easily. Here is a concept about trust that may help deepen your understanding.

## Trust Is Like a Bridge

Trust bridges…

> … are built from both ends.

> … can support lots of traffic.

> … need consistent maintenance.

> … can be severely damaged.

With good "engineers" they can sometimes be repaired, with a lot of effort!

When we talk about broken trust, in adult relationships, most people immediately think of sexual infidelity. We will cover infidelity at the end of this chapter. But first, I'm going to share the five major ways in which we trust.

## 1. LOYALTY

A relationship is like a team. To be a "winning" team, you need to be loyal to each other and know that you can count on your fellow team member. Perhaps you have been at a party when you hear a couple bickering in front of others. It's uncomfortable to hear them make snide remarks, or to make jokes at each other's expense. It is a betrayal of loyalty to each other.

In a healthy relationship, the couple will avoid making each other look bad. They will publicly support each other and settle their differences in private. Here are some questions to ask yourself about a man, when you are trying to determine if he is shows Loyalty:

- Does he correct you in public?

- Will he "watch your back?"

- Does he undermine your decisions?

- Does he make disparaging remarks about you?

- Does he jump in to finish your punch lines?

- Will he throw you under the bus?

## 2. EMOTIONAL TRUST

Having emotional trust means you know you can trust him to be considerate in the way he treats you. An emotionally trustworthy partner will try to avoid hurting your feelings. Healthy couples create a "safe" environment where they can share their tender feelings without criticism. They can be open and vulnerable about their innermost fears and insecurities and know their partner will give them support and understanding. Here are some questions to ask yourself to determine if your man has earned your Emotional Trust.

- Is he considerate of your feelings?

o   When referring to you, is he careful in the words and names he chooses.

o   Does he use your mistakes as ammunition against you in arguments?

o   Do the pet nicknames he uses for you feel good?

o   Does he sincerely apologize if he hurts you?

## 3.  PHYSICAL TRUST

When you trust a man physically, you want him to be gentle and protective. Most men are bigger and stronger than women. A gentleman will use his superior strength to protect women and children. This is not an insult to your own capabilities for self-care. Instead, it is the considerate thing to do. You would do the same for another woman or a child who needs your strength and protection.

For example, he will watch to see if you are cold, and offer his jacket. When you are carrying heavy boxes, he will pick up the biggest one. And when he shakes your hand, it will be firm, but not a hard squeeze that hurts your fingers.

On an intimate level, you need to be able to trust a man physically during sexual activity. It is a sign of his emotional maturity if he shows care and consideration for your physical comfort and satisfaction, not just his climax.

Here is a true story about my husband, Dixon, when he showed me I could trust him with my physical well-being:

*I happen to have fibromyalgia, which means I am extra- sensitive to physical discomfort. My body often hurts as though I have lots of bruises. One of the ways I experience this is by being very sensitive to whether or not the sheets under me are smooth or wrinkled. If they are wrinkled, it feels like I am trying to sleep on rocks. Sometimes I think the story of the "Princess and the Pea" is about a woman with fibromyalgia, who can feel a small pea inserted under many layers of mattresses.*

*Not related to fibromyalgia, I needed to be in the hospital for surgery and a few days of recovery. As you may know, hospitals do not use fitted sheets. Instead, they use flat sheets, and therefore whenever I turned over, the sheets would shift and form wrinkles under me. Since I was already sore from the surgery, the wrinkles made me even more uncomfortable than usual.*

*Well, my sweet husband made arrangements to have a roll-away bed placed next to mine in the hospital. He slept on the roll-away bed for several days. Whenever I needed to turn over, he would stand up and smooth the sheets under me.*

This is just one example of many ways he has shown his trustworthiness to take care of me physically.

Here are some things to consider when seeking an indication of your man's Physical Trustworthiness:

- o Will he protect and care for you physically?

- o Do you observe him being gentle with children and the elderly?

- o Does he ever threaten to hurt you physically?

- o Any form of physical abuse is a betrayal of this trust.

## 4. INTEGRITY

Full integrity is more than being honest, it is deep authenticity. It means that your inside (thoughts, feelings, etc.) match your outside; there's no hidden agenda. For example, if a new man you date "acts" kind and loving, when he secretly just wants to score another mark on his bedpost (an example of immature Wolf behavior), then he has a huge lack of integrity. Integrity also means you can trust him to follow through when he says he'll do something.

I was blessed to be raised by parents who both had high integrity. My mom used to say, "If I tell you

I will be there, then, unless I have a broken leg and can't walk, I will be there." My mom and dad taught me to never make promises unless I was *sure* to keep them. They taught me that if there was any question in my mind about keeping a promise, it was important to explain the possible limitations up front.

For example, my girlfriends may want me to go dancing next Friday night, but I think I may have a heavy day at work. I should explain to them that I *want* to go, but cannot promise until I find out how I feel at the end of my workday.

It's important to set an Integrity boundary with your man.

Explain to him how integrity helps to build trust, and you want to trust him, so he needs to keep his word. You can help him by making it safe for him to tell you his real feelings.

For example, if you want him to take you out this weekend, but you think he may be too tired, you need to allow him to tell you what is real for him, and not try to manipulate him into telling you what you want to hear. Here are some questions to ask yourself about Integrity in your relationship:

o   Do we keep our word?

- o Do we make promises….and then break them for our convenience?

- o If we are not SURE, do we let each other know the possible limitations?

## 5. BASIC HONESTY

Honesty is always the best policy in a good relationship. You need to be able to believe what your man tells you. Although this book is about love relationships, the need for honesty is inherent in every relationship; between employers & employees, between parents & children, between friends & neighbors. If you can't believe someone, you shouldn't trust them.

However, there is a difference between being brutally honest and honestly tactful. For example: If you ask a man if he likes your new dress, and he says, "It makes your butt look fat!" he's just being honest, right? No, he's being brutal and untactful. A more emotionally mature man might say, "You have other dresses that show off your pretty figure better." This is honest *and* tactful.

When you set an expectation (boundary) about the level of honesty you want in your relationships, you need to also ask yourself what level of honesty you personally use. It is hypocritical to expect him to be open and honest with you, if you are dishonest with him.

For example, many people think it is considerate to tell little white lies. They may justify their lies by saying they didn't want to hurt someone's feelings. But, if you have a commitment to honesty, you can always find a way to tell the truth tactfully. Be honest with the little things, and the big things will take care of themselves.

Here are some questions to help you determine the level of Basic Honesty in your relationship:

○ Do we tell the truth to each other?

○ Do we justify using little white lies?

○ Do your friends or co-workers hear you tell lies?

○ Do you ask your friends to lie for you?

If you practice making these five forms of trust a part of the daily way you live, and expect the same standard from the men in your life, it will help build a firm foundation on which you can add other components of a loving, long-term relationship.

## Sarah Loses Trust

Sarah and her man had been committed for a few months, but after their disastrous conversation, she realized that she was no longer feeling as open and trusting as she had initially. The "honeymoon" was over, and he was no longer on his best behavior around her.

When he blew up, she became aware that she hadn't felt comfortable with him for quite some time. In fact, she didn't trust him in most of the five above ways. He had not been loyal toward her, had criticized her to his family and friends. Emotionally she didn't feel safe, because of his explosive temper. Physically, he had never hurt her, but she realized she was actually afraid that he might. And his integrity and honesty were both suspect. She had heard him exaggerate about his income, and she now knew that he wasn't the man he had pretended to be. Sarah decided she wanted this man out of her life.

At first Sarah was angry. Some of her girlfriends encouraged her to create a big scene, perhaps to storm into his work and publicly humiliate him. Or post something really nasty on Facebook for all his friends to see. Knowing that he had previously "tossed her under the bus" to his friends, she assumed he would do so again when they broke up.

But, with coaching, Sarah realized that the person she was angriest with was actually herself. She had allowed her boundaries to be ignored. She had allowed his increasingly bad behavior and not spoken up. She had wanted the "illusion of a relationship" more than her actual happiness. She had learned an important lesson!

Sarah decided to leave the relationship with dignity and class; no nasty FB posts or ugly emails. She even considered writing him a brief "Thank You" note for prompting the growth lesson in her life. Now, if she runs into him at a restaurant (maybe with a new girl), she can stop by their table, smile, and say "Hi."

Perhaps you wonder why I would share a "love" story that doesn't end "happily ever after?" There are several reasons why I think this true story is very important for you.

First, it is a story of Sarah's growth. This path of growth is a common one for most women. Her story shows the stages most of us go through. We gradually learn and get gradually stronger in setting our boundaries, maintaining them, understanding feelings, communicating our needs, and building trust. It is a process. The ability and skills to build a True Love relationship is a life long journey, in which we look for progress, not perfection. Sarah is definitely progressing!

# What About Infidelity?

Can you rebuild a trust bridge after it is severely broken? The answer is: "Yes", "No", and "Maybe. "

It all depends on BOTH of the bridge architects (you & him).

- Do you both think it's worth it?

- Do you have the skills? Or can you develop the skills?

- Can you, as a couple, supply the materials: patience, understanding, and honesty?

- Are you both willing to do the work?

- Are you both willing to put in lots of time and effort?

- Are you both willing to make the commitment?

If you and your man decide you want to rebuild a broken Trust Bridge, here are some steps to take.

First, since this book is written primarily for women, I'm going to assume that he is the one who cheated. Sex is an act of intimacy and when betrayal has happened, it means that an outsider was allowed to trespass inside the boundaries that define you as a couple. After a trust break, caused by infidelity, the main thing that is needed is his commitment to change. Another word for change is repentance.

## The 6 Steps of Change & Healing

### 1. Recognize the Error

His awareness is the first step. He cannot make a change unless he recognizes that he did something wrong. When he is defensive, it blocks his ability to recognize his errors.

### 2. Regret or Remorse

Sincere sorrow for his errors will help motivate him to improve. This is not the same as feeling guilty, which can cause shame or discouragement, and therefore a lack of motivation. It helps if he feels empathy for the hurt he has caused you.

### 3. Resolve and Recommit

When he resolves to change, it may help to "put something behind" his commitment. For example, if he promises to call you every day for a few minutes of "connection" time .... he could agree to wash the dinner dishes for a week if he forgets to call.

Make SMART commitments: Specific and Singular, Measurable and Mutual, Action-Oriented, Realistic and Relevant, and Time-bound.

### 4. Reveal and Ask Forgiveness

An important clarification is that he is "asking for" not "demanding" forgiveness. It is always up to the betrayed person to decide if they want to forgive. Forgiveness is a gift. There is no guarantee of forgiveness.

It is often helpful to find another trusted and responsible person for him to "confess" to. Perhaps this is a best friend, a mentor, a counselor, or a minister. This helps verify that he is truly willing to acknowledge his error.

### 5. Restitution and Repair

He needs to try to repair the damage or hurt that has been caused. For example, if the infidelity was revealed publicly, then it is likely you feel public humiliation and he may need to make a public acknowledgement and apology for his mistakes.

Repair should include a full and complete break with the other woman. Perhaps you want him to tell her (on a phone call on speaker) that he will never again contact her, and he wants her to not contact him in any way. He needs to tell her that he chooses you over her.

Another possibility, if "your" bed was used, you may require a new bed with "clean mattress and sheets."

## 6. Receive Another Chance

Some women's "back stories" make it too painful to risk the possible pain of giving him another chance.

But, if you decide to give him another chance, it is especially important for him to maintain trust in every other area, no matter how small. One form of giving a chance is to use a probation period, to allow him to demonstrate his trustworthiness.

These same six steps can be used to rebuild trust after other major breaks in your Trust Bridge, such as financial issues. It is not easy to rebuild a broken bridge, nor is it easy to build a long-term loving relationship. There will always be challenges. But you *can* do it! If both of you are willing to do the work and be honest about your own thoughts and feelings, together you can overcome the hurdles, and gain the sweet and juicy relationship you deserve. With strong *trust* as a foundation, your loving relationships can last forever, like this bridge!

Please remember that I am here for you. If you are running into challenges that seem too much for you to handle, reach out to me. Send me an email: Angeline@GorillaLove.com.

# Chapter 7:

# "What About Intimacy and Sex?"

*"Only the united beat of sex and heart together, can create ecstasy."*

— Anaïs Nin, Delta of Venus

# Not About the Birds and Bees

This is the X-rated chapter. I'm going to say some things that are graphic and may even seem brutal. This is not the birds and bees and pretty flowers and trees talk about sex. So, here goes.

In an Ideal World, all adults would be emotionally mature; all men would be loving and protective, and all women would be wise and nurturing. Human couples, like ducks, coyotes, and bald eagles, would mate for life and work together to raise happy offspring.

Unfortunately, we are not ducks, nor coyotes, nor bald eagles, and we consistently make bad choices when choosing a mate. We are not usually emotionally mature when we begin partnering, or maybe not for a long while and after a lot of work. So we have problems when it comes to forming relationships, and that translates into problems with sex.

I wish we lived in an Ideal World, but we don't. In today's world, sex can be cheap and easy, with little or no meaning. Might as well be two dogs humping, or wild, screaming monkey sex, after which neither one calls the next morning, because there was really no connection, other than genitals.

At its worst, sex can be a violent expression of hostility that demeans one or both partners; like rape, whether as a random attack, a carefully planned manipulation of an innocent young person, act of war, or as a degrading event between people who are dating or even married. These are all examples of one person's disconnected, criminal disregard for the sanctity of another's physical, emotional and personal space. It is simply using another's body for their own selfish reasons.

But, on the other hand, at its best, sex is the culminating connection for a couple. Rather than an expression of self-gratification, sex becomes a physical expression of generosity and love. It is the most intimate a couple can be, a time to share their tenderest and juiciest love for each other. This is the kind of sex I want for you!

## Is Sexual Chemistry the Key to Relationships?

Unfortunately, sexual chemistry will lie to you! It's like sugar. You look at that big slice of cake while sugar whispers to you, "One little bite won't count," "Well, two won't matter," "You've been good all day, so you deserve this," and "You can do extra treadmill time tomorrow." And, before you know it, you eat the whole slice—and lick the last of the frosting off your plate. You just got sold down the river by a lying glob of sugar!

Did you know that studies have been done in which rats are injected with cocaine until they become addicted? Then the rats are introduced to sugar and given time to develop a taste for it. Finally, the rats are offered a choice—sugar or cocaine—and invariably the rats choose the sugar! Sugar is more addictive than cocaine! And yet, for more than 100 years now, society has said sugar is OK.

Well, I'm here to tell you, you can't trust what society says. And if your temptation is not sugar, then just substitute alcohol, or sexy shoes, or whatever-it-is that dumps those yummy endorphins into your system.

It feels *so* good, and if you are not the master of your physical or emotional drives, those drives will cause you to break your diet, break your budget, or break your commitments, one little lie at a time.

Sexual chemistry can do the same thing! It's so yummy and juicy, it can blind you to red flags, and take over, especially early in relationships. It will whisper to you, "This is love," "This is the real thing," and "He's the one." Then, a short while later (after you've opened yourself to physical and emotional intimacy) you bump into reality—and you realize you have no idea who this guy really is and you start wondering if you made a mistake. You could kick yourself! It's just like the remorse you feel after you eat the cake, or buy that fifth pair of sexy shoes.

Let me tell you what sexual chemistry really is: It's the body's physical drive to perpetuate the species. Yep, it's simply that age-old urge to breed. And generally, your new man feels it even more strongly than you do! It just feels so delicious to press your breasts against his chest, and your hips just ache to snuggle up to his. I swear it's like your hips have a mind of their own!

The sexual chemistry ride is kind of like a car rolling downhill. It's your job to control the speed so that the ride can be enjoyable and you have a safe landing, rather than an adrenaline filled joy ride that ends in a crash!

Patti Stanger of the Millionaire Matchmaker says, "Absolutely no sex until AFTER you've had that important relationship discussion and both make a commitment to monogamy." TV personality, Steve Harvey, agrees, no sex before a minimum of three months. And, although the press scoffs, many cultures and religions practice celibacy until marriage…. with a much lower divorce rate!

So, develop mastery over your sexual chemistry! Don't fall for the false promise of its early and easy acceptance. It's power, though juicy and seductive, can cloud your vision and distort your grasp of what's really happening.

A key indicator of emotional maturity is the ability to delay gratification. Take your time and build a solid foundation first. Get to know him, be curious about what makes him tick. Have patience with him and yourself as you build a bridge of trust.

Then, when it's both physically and emotionally safe, you can take some risks, get off the brakes, and sensibly allow yourself to be vulnerable and open to intimacy.

## What About all the Rules?

There are a lot of books that want to give you *rules* about how to behave to "catch" a man. Most of those rules are about playing games; they're just forms of deceit. They tell you how long you should make him wait when he comes to pick you up, or before you call him back, or how to pretend you are interested in him, etc. Some of those books even give you rules about sex. Some tell you how to act sexy, and even to fake orgasms.

I don't believe in playing games. It leads to false expectations about who you really are. I believe in being authentic. It is the foundation of true intimacy.

## How far should you go on the first date?

Let me ask you– how well can you possibly know him on the first or even second date? It's fairly easy for most men (and women) to show an attractive presentation on a first date. So, he's cute, he says nice things, and you're feeling the chemistry. But, ask yourself this: If it turns out that he's really not who he's making himself out to be, that his initial presentation of himself is false, how will you feel? What if he never calls again? What if he's just a Wolf wanting another conquest? How will you feel tomorrow if you share kisses tonight?

If you're okay with his deceit, don't mind kissing cute jerks, and won't have regrets, then why not share kisses?

Kissing is one thing, but if you are considering having sex on the first date, I say, "No, absolutely not!" It's just not smart to get that physically vulnerable with someone you don't really know. He can easily lie about STDs, not to mention lying about his feelings for you.

And just for clarification, "sexual intimacy" includes any contact with genitals; including oral, manual, or full intercourse. I don't care what Clinton said, if one of you cums, you had sex.

Intimacy = In. To. Me. See.

When we are deeply seen, accepted and loved for who we really are, the relationship is automatically emotionally intimate. You probably have this emotional acceptance with your best girlfriends. When you share deep emotional authenticity (intimacy) with your man it creates the yummiest, juiciest sex ever! You are both open and vulnerable, emotionally and physically. Some people describe sex on this level as spiritual. In the quote at the beginning of this chapter, Anaïs Nin called it ecstasy.

This kind of loving, connected sex, when both partners feel truly safe to be themselves, is the connection we all really want. It's what we are all hungry for. Yes, even the one-night-stand guys and the hook-up girls want it. So, why don't they act like they want real connection? Good question!

## The Hazards of On-Line Dating

Some of the current on-line dating forums encourage short- term, shallow behavior. Tinder, for example, uses an extremely quick prompt for judgement, based on surface appearance, to determine if you are interested. It's just a quick swipe left or right, then a brief text and you're on to the next. This is a virtual playground for self-absorbed men who just want a hook-up. Here are a few quotes from an article by Nancy Jo Sales for *Vanity Fair* magazine, in which she writes about Tinder dating.

http://www.vanityfair.com/culture/2015/08/tind er-hook-up- culture-end-of-dating

*Marty… says he's slept with 30 to 40 women in the last year: "I sort of play that I could be a boyfriend kind of guy," in order to win them over, "but then they start wanting me to care more ... and I just don't."*

*Alex, his friends agree, is a Tinder King, a young man of such deft "text game"— "That's the ability to actually convince someone to do something over text," —he is able to entice young women into his bed on the basis of a few text exchanges..."*

*In February, one study reported there were nearly 100 million people—perhaps 50 million on Tinder alone—using their phones as a sort of all-day, every-day, handheld singles club, where they might find a sex partner as easily as they'd find a cheap flight to Florida.*

Some young women, who are not looking for a long-term commitment at this stage of their lives, may go along with this easy sex behavior. But, I believe there is an inherent problem for women who repeatedly have sex with men without any relationship connection. They block their response to the bonding hormones. Over time, the sexual connection gets devalued. It loses its power, it's so quick and easy and.... cheap. Since there is no real connection in this cheap and easy sex, it's all surface, women aren't receiving what they really need (a sense of bonding). And according to some studies, they may not even get the release of orgasm. Here is another quote from the Tinder article in *Vanity Fair*:

*According to multiple studies, women are more likely to have orgasms in the context of relationships than in uncommitted encounters. More than twice as likely, according to a study done by researchers at the Kinsey Institute and Binghamton University.*

The recent style of on-line dating has encouraged both genders to focus on short-lived and shallow relationships, and that includes quick and easy sex. It's especially interesting to note that the result is an increase in male erectile dysfunction for men, and more women who pretend to have orgasms.

In situations like this, it isn't long before sex partners become so jaded that they no longer believe great sex really exists. It's almost become an urban myth, often replaced by drugs and alcohol in an attempt to fill the empty void.

## Don't Be a Hook-Up Victim!

Do you want to have more and better orgasms? Would you like sex to make you feel more beautiful, more loved? Then don't get caught being a victim to shallow men who just want to use you.

Here is what I believe; women determine the type of treatment they receive, by what they are willing to allow. It is up to you to set your value, by setting your boundaries. Where are the boundaries in a Tinder text at 7pm that results in sex with a stranger at 8pm? If you make it easy for shallow men to have sex with you, then of course they will take advantage. It's not the Wolf's fault if you allow it. Instead, be selective, stay connected with your value, and refuse to be sexually involved in hookups. Could that mean less quick and easy sex for you? Probably. But this is definitely a case of "less is more." Less quantity, but more quality.

Unfortunately, in our current society no one is telling today's singles how to get the truly juicy sex, or the real truth that *great sex is based on a deeply intimate and loving connection*. Instead, we are encouraged to go for instant gratification. We are taught that the goal is the climax, but as in everything else, the joy is in the journey, not the destination. The mistaken belief that the climax is the goal, is what underlies the "slam, bam, thank you Ma'am" type of sex. And then he rolls over and goes to sleep. And she thinks, I could have had a better time by myself!

Centuries ago people learned about sex around the campfire, on the farm, or in small multi-generational homes where children certainly heard and may have seen the adults in sexual activity. Sex was not the taboo subject that it often is today; it was simply a natural part of life.

Today parents are often uncomfortable having "the talk" with their children, or they expect Sex Ed units taught at school to handle it. Sadly, most kids today seem to learn more about sex from stories shared by their peers, which usually include misinformation and few insights about relationships.

The growing prevalence of porn is another source of misinformation, especially for men. Because men tend to be visual, pornography can be very appealing to them. However, porn rarely depicts any type of emotional connection. Often it even shows sexual activity that would be painful or demeaning to most women.

And some studies are showing that the increase of erectile dysfunction is tied to the use of porn. It's another indicator that truly satisfying sex includes emotional connection.

The misinformation in porn is especially damaging when it encourages men to believe that when a woman says "No" she is just playing hard to get, and really means "Yes." This has led to date rapes, where the guy honestly felt unfairly charged when she said it was rape.

On the other hand, romance novels appeal to women. But often the information in romance novels can be just as misleading as pornography. In most stories, the couple is so overcome by sexual chemistry that they fall into bed on very little acquaintance. But the sex is "the best ever" for both of them. He is able to read her mind and know exactly what kind of touch she likes, and of course, he is long and hard and lasts until she has had multiple orgasms.

These stories completely avoid any of the awkwardness of getting acquainted, or learning to speak up for what you do or don't like. Not to mention, in the novels, they both love each other's "scent"—come on, let's get real. People don't always smell good, especially if they're sweaty, and didn't just take a shower.

There is one sure way to overcome the hazards of this kind of cheap and easy connection that leaves you feeling empty and unloved. I want to use the analogy of fast food. It is fast and cheap and often tastes good in the moment. But, although the high amounts of sugar and salt in it cause you to go back for more the next day, it doesn't have the nutrition you need. It leaves you feeling hungry while making you fat. It's addictive in all the wrong ways. The antidote is to carefully choose fresh, organic, whole foods and take the time and energy to prepare healthy meals. You are worth the time and effort it takes to invest in your long-term health.

The same is true with sex and intimacy. Slow down. Take the time and energy to carefully choose men who meet your relationship needs. Quit shopping for good men at the "fast food" marts of on-line dating and singles bars. Those are havens for the cheap and easy guys who will use you and toss you aside like yesterday's pizza box. You deserve relationships that nurture and support the precious person you are. A gourmet meal takes time and skills to prepare, and the same is true of Gourmet Love. And honey, you deserve the good stuff!

## Are Married Men Happier?

Although several studies have shown that married men are happier overall than single men, there is still the perpetual myth that men don't want commitment. They just want to get out there and "sow their oats." They don't want to be tied down to one sex partner. And I do believe that's true…. for shallow, self- absorbed, emotionally immature men!

Unfortunately, there seems to be a lot of that kind of men in the dating world these days. Hopefully, this book is helping you recognize the difference. Enlightened with the knowledge you have gained, you *can* find a man with more emotional maturity, with deeper, long-term values. I promise you they *do* exist! And they are definitely happier married than single. This is one reason married men often appear more attractive than single men… because they're happier!

And one more fact: men re-marry much more quickly than women, in about half the time; on average four years for men, and eight years for women. So don't let any man put you down for your desire to create a committed relationship.

## The Cuddle Hormone

Here's something you may not know about women and sex:

A key hormone released during sex is oxytocin, also known as the cuddle hormone. "This lowers our defenses and makes us trust people more," says Dr. Arun Ghosh, a GP specializing in sexual health at the Spire Liverpool Hospital.

It's also the key to bonding, as it increases levels of empathy. Women produce more of this hormone, although it's not clear why, and this means they are more likely to let their guard down and fall in love with a man after sex.

You can read more at:

http://www.dailymail.co.uk/health/article-2031498/Sex-Why- makes-women-fall-love--just-makes-men-want- MORE.html#ixzz3yZ5lkPzr

Bottom line, what you need to know is that an orgasm is going to make you emotionally vulnerable. It's going to make you *want* to be with him. It's nature's way of helping couples bond.

The truth is women are biologically programmed to want security. It's not just some socialized desire to catch a man. Our genes know we are the future caretakers of the potential results of sexual activity. Just because we use the pill or condoms, our hormones don't stop pushing for committed relationships.

We can and do enjoy sex as much (or even more) than men do. Hopefully you know that women have the potential to be multi-orgasmic, while men only get one shot and then have to wait to rewind. Good sex, for women, creates a naturally stimulated desire to bond... for longer than a one-night hookup.

Good sex, based on the healthy relationship information I've shared with you in this book, is nature's glue that helps hold couples together during rough spots in committed relationships.

## Does familiarity breed contempt?

This is a question I often get, and the answer is, "No." It's not the familiarity that's the problem. If both of you are putting up a false front, always being polite, proper, and politically correct, and avoiding authenticity and vulnerability, then it won't take much time to get tired of each other. There is nothing to sustain a shallow relationship like that. It's like eating vanilla pudding every day. You may like vanilla pudding, but you'll get tired of it eventually.

On the other hand, if you take the time and effort to truly get to know each other, you'll learn each other's weaknesses and strengths. Time will provide opportunities to see if he is accountable for his behavior, and if is he willing to do the work to improve the relationship. If you are both willing to commit to building a safe environment of trust, then you can celebrate the differences you each contribute. Your differences can add variety and spice to the "recipe." In this way, the relationship avoids boredom and you build a foundation of genuine connection from which to launch some real sexual fireworks!

The other question I sometimes get asked is, "Why do relationships lose their sexual chemistry over time?" And the answer is, "The relationships in which both members are constantly growing and sharing authentically do NOT lose their sexual chemistry. No, instead it grows ever sweeter and more delicious."

However, sexual chemistry is not a constant feeling. Neither are any of our other feelings. For example, you don't feel constantly angry, nor constantly happy, nor constantly juiced by sexual chemistry. All feelings ebb and flow, but you can choose to nurture the sexual chemistry.

## How to Keep it Juicy

Make it part of your day to do sweet things for each other, send a text or make a phone call. Spice it up with a variety of types of date nights. Have dinner at home with candlelight every now and then. Get some new lingerie. Be playful. Talk with each other about your fantasies. A yummy relationship requires your time and attention, just like planning a yummy dinner menu. The key to keeping the sexual chemistry alive over the years is the same as the key to intimacy. Create an environment where it feels safe to be authentic, be real and share. Then get curious and get to deeply know each other.

In John Gottman's book, *The Seven Principles for Making Marriage Work*, he explains that getting to know each other is an ongoing process, which keeps the marriage alive. His excellent book even has activities to use on date nights, with questions to ask each other to help you get connected.

Some people think the grass is greener on the other side. But, the truth is, the grass is greener wherever you water it.

For example, if you want better health, then do what it takes by focusing on diet and exercise. If you want better finances, then take some budget classes or hire a financial manager. And, if you want more sexual chemistry, then do what it takes. Start by making yourself *feel* sexy. Maybe that means always putting a little make-up on in the morning, or wearing red undies under your jeans, or a daily touch of perfume. Be willing to initiate. Compliment him. All of these are things *you* can do.

But there are two people involved, however, so get curious and ask him what he thinks would improve the sexual chemistry between the two of you.

## Sarah Decides to Wait

When her man started showing his Crab aspect and criticizing her, Sarah realized she had moved into commitment too quickly. When she tried to explain herself, he would often interrupt and sometimes yell at her. To try to "save the relationship," Sarah began holding back her true thoughts and feelings. Naturally, she started losing the loving feelings she had initially felt. She no longer trusted him emotionally, so she pulled back and the intimacy was lost.

Now Sarah realizes she moved into sexual intimacy too soon with this relationship. She understands the value of getting to know a man more fully before committing herself emotionally or sexually.

Sarah wants to be sure her next relationship will have a firm foundation before she allows herself to be so vulnerable to a man. She wants to know that she can trust him in all five ways before she opens her heart and body. She wants to build a life-long Love Affair!

As L'Oreal says, "You're Worth It!"

Ultimately, I believe that it's the women who are in control. Yes, it will take more time and effort to find the good guys. But, hey, you don't go to Ross and buy the first dress you see on the rack... and expect it to be a designer original. So why would you expect to take one minute to swipe right on Tinder, and find an emotionally healthy man? When you want to find the perfect dress, you are willing to spend days shopping, trying on lots of different options, maybe even bringing home a few to show your friends, right?

And, you are even willing to send back a few rejects, because they just don't make you feel beautiful, right? So, be willing to spend at least the same amount of time and effort to find a good man. When you find a man who "fits" your preferences and complements you, he will make you feel every bit as beautiful as the right dress can. And I agree, You Are Worth It!

For more information, go to www.GorillaLove.com. If you would like some relationship coaching, send an email to Angeline@GorillaLove.com to learn about our system for identifying your Ideal Man and building a True Love relationship. I've helped many others and I would love to help you, too! It is my passion to help as many women as possible to have happy and healthy relationships.

# Chapter 8:

# Are You Sure You Want a Committed Relationship?

*"We need to reshape our own perception of how we view ourselves. We have to step up as women and take the lead."*

— Beyoncé

# Maybe You Don't "Need" a Man

I've shared a lot of information about how to recognize an Ideal Man, and how to build healthy relationships. But sometimes women don't really *want* a committed relationship. I want you to know it's okay. It's much more important for you to have a strong and happy relationship with yourself, than to pair off with a man.

In fact, I would say that a good relationship with yourself is primary, before you start building a relationship with your Ideal Man. I consider it a "success" when clients reach the point where they are happy with themselves and realize they don't "need" a man! Eventually, most women decide they "want" a long-term loving relationship, but that's different than "needing" one.

When coaching a new client, I sometimes ask women to give me five reasons they want a committed relationship *and* five reasons they *don't* want one. They are often very surprised to think they might have some reasons they don't want a committed relationship. But, it usually takes only a minute or two, and a couple of questions from me, before they realize they actually have numerous reasons they may be avoiding a committed relationship.

The reality is that most women have avoidance issues to some degree, but they are still fully capable of a committed relationship, if that's what they *really* want.

## Maybe You Are Avoiding

Here are some of the relationship avoidance reasons I often hear, and the reasons that are probably behind each of these statements.

**1 - I'm afraid I'll be hurt. What if he doesn't *really* love me? He might leave me, betray me, cheat on me, abuse me, etc.**

This fear is usually based on my clients' past experiences. Perhaps she has been treated badly by her father, boyfriend, or ex-husband? Maybe all three? Her lack of trust may have served her as a survival strategy in the past. Therefore, it is hard for her to trust men.

Unfortunately, as I've previously mentioned, many women have grown up in dysfunctional families, with abusive, neglectful, or absent fathers. They may have observed their mother being ineffective in handling the physical or emotional abuse dealt to her, or to the children. It may also be that the boys in the family followed in their father's footsteps, adopting similar patterns of abuse. Some women grow up surrounded by examples of men behaving badly.

Often a facet of this poor behavior is men blaming others, particularly women, for their own bad behavior. For example, a dysfunctional father may say to his wife, "If you'd cook a decent meal, I'd be home on time to eat it." With this statement, he is both criticizing her cooking and blaming her for his tardiness, rather than being accountable for managing his own time. With a steady diet of abusive examples growing up, a young girl is likely to carry negative residual effects into womanhood, thinking that's the way all men are. No wonder she has doubts about whether or not she wants a relationship.

Next, let's talk about the following items 2, 3, 4, and 5 in the list of avoidances.

The theme is control. In each case, the woman is concerned that she might lose some form of control in her life. Men have the same fear of losing control in relationships. This is especially true now that women and men are getting married at an older age. They have already established a life for themselves, and don't want to make changes in it to please someone else.

Although men have traditionally been more likely than women to remarry after divorce, recent studies show this gap has narrowed. I believe this change is due to today's women feeling they have a greater right to define themselves and what they are willing to give in a relationship. They are less likely to allow someone else to control them.

When I am coaching women who have control issues, it is usually because they were over-controlled in the past. Perhaps they observed a pattern at home, where females were not given equal opportunities. Through coaching, I help these women to see how times have changed and that they can create a new pattern for themselves.

Among divorced women, I used to see a high percentage of women who have no desire to remarry. They seemed to feel their life had been controlled by their previous partner and they didn't want anything to do with another relationship like that.

These women often said things similar to items #2 through #5.

**2 - I like my privacy and I don't want to have to share my (house, bathroom, bedroom, car, etc.).**

This pertains to different needs for privacy. Some of us are very communal and feel at ease openly sharing everything. But most of us are more limited in our comfort zones. Perhaps as a child we "had" to share everything, and now we finally want to have our own "separate" spaces. Or maybe, we were an only child and didn't have to share anything, so now sharing feels like an invasion of personal space. Again, this is resolved through compassionate respect for one another and skillful communication, which can be learned in relationship coaching.

**3 - I've worked hard to build my career and I don't want to have to share my money.**

This is about how the money will be controlled. With more and more women earning an income and moving up the career ladder, it is common for women to have their own bank and investment accounts. These women often maintain their own individual accounts even after entering a committed relationship.

Instead of combining all their assets, as couples usually did in the past, today's couples create a new joint account into which they each make deposits. The amount of each person's deposit may be determined by a percentage, depending on the income of each partner. This joint account is then used for paying the joint bills such as rent, utilities, home insurance, groceries, etc. On the other hand, individual accounts are maintained to cover personal items such as clothing, grooming expenses, and maybe even a personal car.

**4 - I like my autonomy and don't want to have to answer to anyone else.**

For those who want to maintain their autonomy, today's couples function as equals in a relationship, neither partner has to "answer" to the other. Each person has the right to direct his or her own life. It seems most couples are together these days because they want to "share" their lives to achieve some common goals. Being able to balance individual autonomy with couple harmony is usually based in good communication skills. For most of us, this is often like learning a foreign language. In relationship coaching, I spend a good deal of time on helping my client develop communication skills.

**5 - I don't want to have to clean up after him (dishes, laundry, etc.).**

It used to automatically be the women's responsibility to maintain a clean and tidy home. And the truth is, women are more likely to be affected by home aesthetics. In previous generations, women would just get frustrated when cleaning up after a man. Today's woman feels more comfortable laying a foundation of equal expectations for each partner to clean up after themselves.

**6 – I'm insecure about my appearance and don't want him to see me (naked, in the morning, when I'm sick, etc.).**

Most women can relate to this one to some extent. Men are very visual and studies have shown that men are subconsciously attracted to women who have a noticeable difference between their waist and hip measurements (think Playboy). However, although men are visually attracted to those measurements, in reality, most men "select" women based on the energy the women project. For example, most men are drawn toward women who appear friendly and open...no matter what their measurements are! One study discovered that men's worst fear (regarding women) is that they will be laughed at. Many men feel very vulnerable when approaching women. The point I'm making, is that although *you* may worry about how you look, he is actually more concerned about how you are reacting toward him. Are you smiling and friendly? Does he feel safe that you won't reject him?

**7 - What if he's not "the one" and I meet someone else I like better?**

This avoidance reason is commonly attributed to men, but some women fear it too. I've got to say that I kind of like this one, because it flies in the face of the misconception that there is only one "right" man for you. Instead, there are actually many possibilities. I think this tends to be a factor when women have "settled" rather than actually chosen a man they love. If they love him, and then use the principles in this book to build the relationship, it is highly unlikely they will wander. Instead they will feel a greater loyalty to their man.

### 8 - I think I'm still "in love" with someone else.

It would certainly be hard to be open to building a relationship with a new man when you still love another. In this case, I would coach the woman to see if she can find resolution with the man she loves. Why isn't she with him? Are there issues that could be resolved?

### 9 - Staying in shape and looking good is important to me, but what if he (gets fat, loses his hair, etc.)?

This is a tough one, a double-edged sword, you might say. Many men feel the same way about women. Some men, in fact, keep gathering trophy wives, one after the other for this very reason. This is usually an example of a man's preoccupation with surface appearances, rather than actually loving a woman. Woman can be preoccupied with surface appearance as well. They may feel their partner's appearance is a reflection on them. In either case, men or women, may need to do a little work on self-esteem and boundary setting.

### 10 - My past partner died and now I'm afraid I might be "abandoned" again.

The truth is that most women outlive the man in their life. But maybe this man died exceptionally young, or in a particularly traumatic way. She may actually have some PTSD about the unexpected loss. It needs to be dealt with, so that she can move forward.

Rather than thinking you *have* to have a man in your life, give yourself permission to feel okay about yourself if you choose to avoid a relationship. However, sometime in the future, you may find resolution to some of the avoidances presented above, and then you may feel comfortable to move toward developing a long-term loving relationship with an Ideal Man.

## Sarah Feels Beautiful

This is the stage Sarah is in now, she no longer "needs" a man. She has become stronger and more grounded in the higher value she places in herself. She feels empowered. She has learned to create balance between her Emotional Child and Critical Parent. She feels better about herself. Sarah even feels beautiful, without needing a man to tell her she is.

Ironically, self-assured confident women, at this juicy stage of personal development, tend to attract more men, especially emotionally mature men. Sometimes you hear women say that Mr. Right showed up when they quit looking for him. The law of attraction has been at work. It's because a happy well-balanced woman is like a magnet. It doesn't mean that Sarah can stay at home and expect her Ideal Man to come knocking at her door. No, instead she will go about her life, participating in activities she enjoys, keeping her eyes open to "recognize" the type of man she wants.

Sarah's changed, however. Her growing sense of her own unique value in the world is rapidly crowding out the feelings of inadequacy and desperation of her past. Sarah is beginning to see a bright future ahead for herself.

Sarah is continuing coaching, because she knows that when she begins another relationship, challenges will arise and she will want some help in using her new skills. It is both my privilege and pleasure to help her! And I would feel the same joy in helping you!

I sincerely hope this book brings new insights and relationship skills into your life. It is my deepest desire to help all women build healthy long-term loving relationships! For an opportunity to have a free session, please go to my website: www.GorillaLove.com.

# Chapter 8

# Chapter 9:

# So, How Do I Apply All These Skills?

*"To say that one waits a lifetime for his soulmate to come around is a paradox. People eventually get sick of waiting, take a chance on someone, and by the art of commitment become soulmates, which takes a lifetime to perfect."*

—Criss Jami, Venus in Arms

In this final chapter, I'm going to share several stories to show examples of how to apply all the skills in this book as a relationship develops.

## You are like a Garden

Recently, a client and I were talking about the process of personal growth. An important step, before you get into a relationship, is to get to a place where you really like yourself. She asked me, "But, how do you do that?"

As I thought about it, this analogy occurred to me: Learning to love yourself is like growing a garden. When you look at the dirt, unless you are a farmer, you aren't impressed with the dirt. But you need to spend time working with the dirt, adding compost, adding fertilizer, and maybe even some worms to keep the dirt loose. At this point, depending on what kind of fertilizer you used, your garden is probably kind of "stinky."

Next, you spend some time choosing what you're going to plant. You carefully put the seeds in the ground and water them. But the garden still looks bare. There is nothing to love about this patch of dirt.

Even though it looks unattractive, your garden needs you to lovingly care for it every day! So you put in a lot more time and effort watering daily, and pulling any tiny weeds before they start to take over.

Finally, you see some little green sprouts poke their heads above the dirt. At this point, you may start to like your garden. You may even think it's cute. Please note that you have already put in lots of labor, plenty of time, and a fair bit of expense.

As your garden grows, and you continue to nurture it, you will get excited about each new stage. You brag to your friends and post pictures on Facebook. When you finally begin harvesting, you will proudly serve salads to your friends, made entirely from the produce of your garden. You will share tomatoes and zucchini with the neighbors. And you will swap stories of the challenges you experienced along the way. By this time, you *love* your garden!

If you were raised in a healthy, loving family, your parents spent lots of time, effort and expense supporting your growth.

They provided a healthy environment for you. They "watered and fertilized" by providing good nutrition and education. They weeded, by removing the influences that could be harmful to you, as best they could. And they proudly recorded videos of your first steps for posterity, gradually followed by those of your first soccer games, prom, and graduation. And they loved sharing stories with their friends about the challenges of raising you. Their love for you convinced you that you are lovable!

But, if you were a little seed that "fell by the wayside, or among thorns" and you didn't get that love and nurturing, then you didn't get the necessary support that let you know you are lovable. You may have felt like plain, bare dirt.

Here is where a coach is invaluable. I am like a farmer who can recognize the value in bare dirt. I can see your potential, and I can help you plant and nurture your own garden. I will gently walk you through the steps of fertilizing and weeding, by teaching you mature relationship skills. And gradually, as you peek above the dirt and start to see the sunshine, I will help you recognize and acknowledge each forward step you take. I will help you celebrate your first harvest as you share your "fruit" with others. Like growing a garden, the process of "growing yourself" will bring you to a place of love for yourself!

## Jillena Recognizes Her Ideal Man

This morning I was chatting with my second daughter, Jillena, who lives across the street from me now, with her husband and two young children. We were talking about this book, and she suggested I include some stories about her dating and courtship experiences.

Because I believe good relationships are central to a happy life, I have been very involved in helping each of my three children identify the qualities they wanted in their future spouses. Over the years, I have followed up by giving them support in building strong and loving relationships.

I should mention that after they reach 18, I do avoid getting in my children's "space" unless they invite me. As a parent, I respect my children's right to create their own path, including making mistakes without receiving criticism or uninvited suggestions from me.

Jillena reminded me that I was very instrumental in helping her recognize that Scott was her Ideal Man (and he really is!).

Although Jillena is very attractive, and many men were drawn to her, she experienced most of the same struggles all women go through in finding an Ideal Man. Her plan had been to get married by age 21 and start a family right away. She really wanted to be a wife and mother. Her sister, Kitty, who is only one year older, was already married and had two kids, when Jillena was headed toward 30. Here is a story about her dating experiences.

*Jillena dated a lot, and met a bunch of guys that weren't right for her. The years went by and she was getting really discouraged. Several times I had suggested that her longtime friend, Scott, might be right for her, but she said she didn't think he was interested in her romantically. They were just friends.*

*Jillena called me one day to report her frustration with still another Mr. Wrong. I suggested we create a little quiz to help her identify what she really wanted in a man. I wanted her to move away from her emotional reactions, and stop being influenced by the superficial qualities in the men she was dating. I wanted her to take a deeper look for the qualities that really mattered to her. This was actually the pre-cursor to creating The Gorilla Quiz.*

*All good relationships are based on similar qualities, whether they are romantic relationships or just your friends and family. This means you can gain valuable insight from looking at any long term relationship that is satisfying to you.*

*I had Jillena list her three best girlfriends, and tell me what qualities made those relationships work for her: a sense of humor, emotional honesty, and spirit of adventure were among her answers. Then, I had her list her brother and a few other male friends. She named qualities that made each of those relationships work. Together, we created a list of 10 qualities.*

*Next, I had her create a spreadsheet with the list of 10 qualities down the left side, and the list of her friends and family across the top. Then I had her rate each quality for each person on a 1- 3 scale, with 1 being low and 3 being high. At the bottom, she totaled each person's score. This gave her a*

*benchmark for what worked for her in relationships.
Like this:*

|   |                      | Sally | June | Cecelia | Doug | Don | Carli |
|---|----------------------|-------|------|---------|------|-----|-------|
| 1 | Emotionally Honest   | 2     | 3    | 1       | 2    | 1   | 3     |
| 2 | Sense of Humor       | 1     | 2    | 3       | 3    | 2   | 1     |
| 3 | Ambitious            | 3     | 1    | 2       | 1    | 3   | 2     |
| 4 | Handles Money        | 2     | 2    | 3       | 2    | 2   | 1     |
| 5 | Spiritual            | 1     | 2    | 3       | 3    | 1   | 2     |
| 6 | Few Addictions       | 3     | 3    | 1       | 1    | 2   | 2     |
| 7 | Does the little things | 3   | 1    | 2       | 2    | 2   | 3     |
| 8 | Adventurous          | 1     | 2    | 3       | 2    | 3   | 1     |
| 9 | Wants Kids           | 2     | 3    | 1       | 2    | 1   | 3     |
| 10| Good Family Values   | 1     | 2    | 3       | 3    | 2   | 2     |

| Total | 19 | 21 | 22 | 21 | 19 | 20 |
|---|---|---|---|---|---|---|

*Next I had her list several of the Mr. Wrongs she had dated, like this:*

| | | Jack | Bob | Owen | Bill |
|---|---|---|---|---|---|
| 1 | Emotionally Honest | 1 | 2 | 1 | 2 |
| 2 | Sense of Humor | 2 | 1 | 1 | 3 |
| 3 | Ambitious | 1 | 1 | 2 | 1 |
| 4 | Handles Money | 2 | 1 | 1 | 1 |
| 5 | Spiritual | 1 | 2 | 1 | 1 |
| 6 | Few Addictions | 1 | 2 | 2 | 2 |
| 7 | Does the little things | 2 | 1 | 1 | 1 |
| 8 | Adventurous | 1 | 3 | 2 | 2 |
| 9 | Wants Kids | 1 | 1 | 3 | 3 |

| 10 | Good Family Values | 2 | 2 | 1 | 1 |
|---|---|---|---|---|---|
| | Total | 14 | 16 | 15 | 17 |

*Jillena looked at the above grid, saw how all the "wrong" men had scored several points below her friends and family, and said, "No wonder those guys weren't right for me!"*

*Then I said, "How about Scott? Let's rate him." She started down the list, "Okay, honest 3, humor 3, ambitious 3, money 3, and spiritual 3....aw, shit, Mom!" She got it! She recognized he could be her Ideal Man.*

| | | Scott |
|---|---|---|
| 1 | Emotionally Honest | 3 |
| 2 | Sense of Humor | 3 |
| 3 | Ambitious | 3 |
| 4 | Handles Money | 3 |
| 5 | Spiritual | 3 |

| | | |
|---|---|---|
| 6 | Few Addictions | 2 |
| 7 | Does the little things | 3 |
| 8 | Adventurous | 3 |
| 9 | Wants Kids | 2 |
| 10 | Good Family Values | 3 |
| | Total | 28 |

*Jillena's view of Scott changed when she perceived who he really was. She then changed her attitude and the way she related to him. She let him know she was interested in being more than just friends. Jillena was surprised to find that he was actually interested in her, too.*

*Scott is a man who likes to take his time and not rush into things, so he was waiting to see if she was interested. Please note that many men are cautious about being vulnerable and acting on the attractions they feel. You may be missing some of the men who are interested in you! But now that Jillena let Scott know she was interested, they began dating.*

*Several months into their committed dating, Jillena needed to have her wisdom teeth removed. Unfortunately, she had some severe complications, and needed to be on heavy medications and stay in bed for several days. She called Scott to tell him how sick she was. Although he lived several hours away from her, he volunteered to come and take care of her.*

*He went to the video store to get DVDs she would enjoy, picked up popsicles at the grocery store, and woke her up on time to take her medications. Although she looked terrible, and there was nothing in it for him, he tenderly took care of her.*

*One day, they were sitting on the sofa watching a video. She was leaning against his chest, with a small towel to catch the drool. Jillena realized this was a man who would truly "be there" for her. Someone she could trust. She realized she loved him! And she made a decision to commit to him. Even though he hadn't proposed, she got his name tattooed over a small heart. (Of course, I don't actually recommend this.)*

Things to notice:

1. Jillena took lots of time to get to know Scott, they had been friends for several years.

2. She also looked deeper than the surface by using the Quiz to identify what she really wanted.

3. She used a period of "exclusive" dating to get to know him better, even before she knew she was in love.

4. She observed his behavior was not just self-centered. He could generously give his time, energy, and focus to her.

5. Only after doing her due diligence did she commit to him.

## Jillena and The Motorcycle

*After Jillena and Scott committed to each other, it was almost a year before they were married. He was living and working in San Francisco, and she was in San Diego, but he came to visit her as often as he could. Jillena had a red convertible and a motorcycle, which she loved. Since her apartment did not include a garage, she always chained her motorcycle to a nearby telephone pole. While Scott was in town, if they needed to go separate ways, he would drive one vehicle and she the other.*

*One weekend, Scott had to leave while Jillena was still at work. When she got home, she found the chain around the telephone pole, but no motorcycle. In Scott's rush to grab a cab to meet his plane, she concluded, he had apparently forgotten to chain up her bike. It had been stolen! She was furious!*

*Jillena was fuming when she called me! She had prepared an angry message, which she wanted to send to Scott, but she called to ask my advice first. I suggested she needed to have compassion, because in this early stage of their relationship, they were setting the patterns for their future communications. I reminded her that a time would come when she would make a big mistake, and she would want him to have compassion for her.*

*Even though she might never have an opportunity to replace the motorcycle, I asked her which was more important to her: the bike or the relationship? "Remember," I said, "that you should always assume a positive intention. Scott loves you and he wouldn't intentionally lose your bike, so he probably had some kind of challenge."*

*Although it was hard, she started calming down. Later that evening, when she was fully calm, she called Scott. With loving voice tones, she asked him, "Honey, when I got home, the chain was around the telephone pole, but my motorcycle is missing. Do you know what happened?"*

*"Sure" Scott said, "I dropped it off at the mechanics to have the brakes fixed. You can pick it up tomorrow."*

Over the years, Jillena has used the "secrets" I have shared in this book. Frequently she still calls to ask me for advice. (Everyone can use a good coach!) She and Scott have been married almost 13 years now, and have two kids. Their relationship is hot and juicy! They have regular date nights, and get away for mini-vacations every few months.

Because their love is based on the deeper qualities they really value, their love grows. They have created a safe environment where they can share their true thoughts and feelings, thus the intimacy grows, and the sexual chemistry naturally grows too. And as an added benefit, they're setting a good example for their kids.

Key learning from this story:

1. Assume a positive intention.

2. Calm down before conversing about an emotional subject.

3. Seek first to understand before being understood.

4. Use gentle voice tones.

5. Check in with your coach.

## When I Met My Husband

Here is my own story.

*When I met Dixon, he had been a bachelor for 17 years, after a failed five-year marriage. He told me he would never get married again, didn't like kids or organized religion, and had been unfaithful with every woman he had been with. He called himself a "skirt chasing fool." But underneath this emotionally immature bad-boy, I recognized a tender and loving man who really wanted a different life than the shallow one he was living.*

*His father had been emotionally abusive, and Dixon was disconnected from his family. After Dixon's honorable discharge from the Army in 1967, he got involved in the drugs and free love scene.*

*During this time, he also got married and had a son. Due to drug and alcohol abuse, Dixon's life went downhill for a time. He eventually found himself in Nevada one day, unaware of where he was. Dixon voluntarily entered a residential drug rehab program where he stayed for the next seven years. Over time, he eventually became Vice President of the program.*

*During his time in rehab, Dixon got divorced. His ex-wife and son moved to another state. Although Dixon remained on amicable terms with his ex, he rarely saw his son, nor did he build a strong connection with him. Dixon didn't know how to build connections. But he did pay his child support consistently.*

*After leaving the rehab program, Dixon's life still had an empty void—which he attempted to fill with alcohol and one-night stands. He was living the free and easy life touted by many bachelors. But underneath, he felt alone and unhappy, so he looked for a new way to improve his life. Dixon put himself into group therapy, which he continued for eleven years. He learned some psychological principles and some skills around processing emotions.*

*By the time I met him, Dixon had quit smoking and drinking, but due to his dysfunctional background, he still didn't know to build healthy connections. He'd had a series of girlfriends, but couldn't maintain a relationship. I have no doubt these women cared about this lovable man. One clue is that at least five of them came to our wedding. I suspect they wanted to see what kind of woman managed to get him to settle down. I'm sure they were surprised to see a mother with three kids and a religious background.*

*Dixon and I had many long talks about deep subjects. A high priority for me in a man is his ability to "process" the emotional challenges of life. As I've previously mentioned, my mother was a psychologist, and our family conversations were filled with references to building trust, managing boundaries, and maintaining positive attitudes. Like me, Dixon could "talk the talk."*

*What couldn't be seen on the outside of our marriage was our emotional connection. Although Dixon didn't have the full set of skills to build and maintain a relationship, I did—all the skills I have shared with you in this book. And I needed all of them!*

*Building a relationship with an emotionally damaged and emotionally immature man is not easy! It is very challenging! Every long-term loving relationship takes a lot of work and commitment. But, the result is so worth it. I adore my husband! He has become the perfect man for me. Our relationship grows sweeter and juicier every day! As for sex, even though we are getting "old" I swear it's better now than 25 years ago, when we met.*

Unfortunately, most of the men you meet are carrying emotional damage, or baggage of some kind. You will need to learn and practice all the skills in this book, so that you have them readily available when you finally recognize your Ideal Man, and wish to constructively resolve the inevitable challenges he brings...and the ones you bring to him, too!

The point I'm making by sharing this story is, your Ideal Man will probably not be Ideal when you first meet him. He probably won't look like Magic Mike, or dress like the guys in GQ. And you probably won't have seven orgasms the first time you have sex. But, if you have learned to recognize the right Man-imal for you, underneath his possible emotional immaturity, you can find your Ideal Man.

Did you catch some of the clues in Dixon's story that told me he was a quality man, with potential to be my Ideal?

For example:

1. He was willing to be accountable for his personal growth, as shown by putting himself in rehab and group therapy.

2. He showed commitment by staying in each of those programs for a long period of time.

3. He maintained good terms with his ex, which demonstrates his loving heart, rather than being bitter or blameful.

4. He showed responsibility by paying child support consistently.

5. He quit alcohol, drugs and smoking, thus showing his ability to overcome addictions.

All of these are ways in which Dixon *was* emotionally mature, or working toward it, and these traits and actions told me he was very workable as a mate, even though he appeared self-centered and emotionally immature in other ways.

I want to point out that I did not "catch" Dixon, nor did I "train" him. He is his own man, and he made the choice to marry a woman with kids at home (whom he has grown to love). And all along the way, he has made his own choices to grow within the relationship. Sometimes his choices were based on boundaries I set, but it was never a case of me being his trainer, or boss, or even coach. We are equals and each bring a unique set of strengths and weaknesses to our relationship. Neither is better than the other. We have built our marriage as a team. We both want what is best for each of us individually (center circle), and together (win/win).

When you recognize your Ideal Man, and you both take the time and effort to commit to building your future, you *can* have a long-term True Love relationship. Together you can lovingly support each other by setting healthy boundaries, building trust, sharing vulnerable feelings, and communicating authentically.

I don't know how to tell you how very much I would like to support you in recognizing a good man and building a long-term True Love relationship. I believe your greatest happiness in life will be found in a healthy, loving relationship. I hope you will use this book, refer to it often, learn and practice the skills.

For some people, reading a self-help book is all the support they need. But other people learn best when they can talk with someone and personally share their situations and challenges. If you would like to work with me, please send me an email: Angeline@GorillaLove.com.

And please post a review of this book on Amazon. When women share their wisdom, we can all benefit!

# Chapter 9

# The Gorilla Quiz

If you have access to a computer or cell phone, I highly recommend you use it to take The Gorilla Quiz, because it will automatically tally the scores for you. If not, you can use this list of questions and put your answers on the Answer Sheet. Have fun!

1.  He brags that all women find him attractive.

2.  He has a need to control others and always be in charge.

3.  He is highly ambitious, works hard, focused on achieving financial success.

4.  He is dedicated to extensive workouts and bodybuilding.

5.  He is extra picky about his grooming; keeps himself, his car and his home immaculate.

6.  He loves extreme sports: participates in downhill skiing, para-gliding, car racing, etc.

7.  He is always willing to party and is often the social organizer.

8. He is very well-read and likes to discuss ideas.

9. He is involved with social issues: Greenpeace, Occupy Wall Street, climate change, etc.

10. He is accepting and non-critical, therefore others around him feel good about themselves.

11. He looks for flaws in everyone and everything, and makes negative comments either compulsively or to feel superior.

12. He avoids being accountable for his own negative results, thinks it was just bad luck, or even that others are out to get him.

13. He can be romantic and focused on pleasing you; there are candles, flowers, flattering words, etc.

14. He is drawn to power careers, i.e. politician, manager of a company, in the military, or police force.

15. He feels he must have the best of everything: car, house, boat, watch, clothes, etc.

16. He knows carb and calorie counts of many foods and may drink protein shakes, etc.

17. The ambience of his environment is important to him and he works to make it attractive.

18. He gets a rush from performing on center stage, as a musician, public speaker, etc.

19. He has a large group of friends. He's the guy everyone invites, cuz he's so *fun*!

20. He is highly educated, and tends to expand his knowledge through intellectual pursuits.

21. He has high ideals for society, works to make improvements and votes accordingly.

22. Children are comfortable with him. His kids (and the neighborhood kids?) think he's their buddy.

23. He often criticizes others and sees himself as knowing what's best, not only for himself but everyone else.

24. He blames others for his poor performance or circumstance: teachers, parents, society, etc.

25. He measures his masculinity by the number of women he's "had."

26. He is tenacious and determined to have things his own way. "My way or the highway."

27. He is highly competitive (rather than collaborative) and driven to be at the top.

28. He is willing to make other the "butt" of his jokes, especially smaller or gay men, women, or

individuals with lower perceived status than himself.

29. He is drawn toward visually aesthetic careers, such as artist, interior design, or architecture.

30. He is adventurous and likes to travel (backpack?) to exotic locations.

31. He is easy going, can be a goofball, very playful, and may seem immature.

32. He is more a thinker than a physical do-er.

33. He is committed to charitable or religious causes. Donates his time and/or resources accordingly.

34. He is very tactile and cuddly. He is comfortable with holding hands or other PDAs with his female partner.

35. He judges others and/or gathers knowledge about people, so thinks he is in a position to judge.

36. He thinks he is the victim of others' bad intentions.

37. He tends to see women as sexual objects, rather than as human beings with depth or agency.

38. He can be a bully, get impatient and lack empathy for others, especially if he perceives weakness.

39. He is generally in a business career, and usually in a suit and tie.

40. He wears clothing to show off his physical build: tight T shirts, sleeveless tanks, etc.

41. He is unusually good looking, like a model or an actor. He may even seem gay or metrosexual because of his grooming habits.

42. He always wants to try some new or exciting challenge.

43. He has a friendly sense of humor. Can play jokes on others, but never mean-spirited, just silly.

44. He gravitates toward intellectual careers: teacher, lawyer, writer, philosopher, etc.

45. He is spiritual or religious and may be a seeker or adhere to the teachings of a group.

46. He is very masculine; down-to-earth, a natural man's man. He is comfortable with who he is and makes no pretenses.

47. He is willing to put others down in an effort to make himself look better, get attention, etc.

48. He gets in trouble often: gets fired, arrested, tickets, fights, conflicts, lawsuits, etc.

49. He may have had sexual harassment charges against him.

50. He thinks he "owns" his woman; she should dress, do, be, and say what he says.

51. He can be greedy and willing to benefit financially even when it creates a loss for others.

52. He and his buddies are into physical sports: football, martial arts, boxing, hockey, etc.

53. He has an extensive wardrobe and enjoys using a lot of accessories; watches, bracelets, scarves, hats, etc.

54. He is an adrenaline junkie and likes to push the limits.

55. Although he has many friends, he may actually be lonely, due to lack of deep connections.

56. He is very intelligent and may be seen as witty or a "nerd."

57. He is idealistic; may even seem self-righteous to others who do not share his high ideals.

58. He works with his hands, may be working in a blue collar job: mechanic, cowboy, farmer, construction, etc.

59. He is a perfectionist and overly demanding of everyone, without genuine appreciation for the efforts or support.

60. He is often angry and hostile, and thinks he "deserves" better treatment, circumstances, or recognition.

## Scoring the Gorilla Quiz

For each question, give your man a score of 0, 1, 2, or 3.

0 = nothing like him.

1 = a little bit like him.

2 = a lot like him.

3 = yes, that is him!

Then add the numbers ACROSS into the TOTAL box on the right.

The highest total is your man's main Man-imal aspect. Be sure to also take a look at his scores in Rat and Crab. In addition, you may want to go to my website and take The Maturity Quiz. It is free.

# The Gorilla Quiz

| | | | | | | | | Total | |
|---|---|---|---|---|---|---|---|---|---|
| 1 | | 13 | | 25 | | 37 | | 49 | | | Wolf |
| 2 | | 14 | | 26 | | 38 | | 50 | | | Pit-Bull |
| 3 | | 15 | | 27 | | 39 | | 51 | | | Shark |
| 4 | | 16 | | 28 | | 40 | | 52 | | | Rhino |
| 5 | | 17 | | 29 | | 41 | | 53 | | | Panther |
| 6 | | 18 | | 30 | | 42 | | 54 | | | Monkey |
| 7 | | 19 | | 31 | | 43 | | 55 | | | Panda |
| 8 | | 20 | | 32 | | 44 | | 56 | | | Owl |
| 9 | | 21 | | 33 | | 45 | | 57 | | | Lion |
| 10 | | 22 | | 34 | | 46 | | 58 | | | Gorilla |
| 11 | | 23 | | 35 | | 47 | | 59 | | | Crab |
| 12 | | 24 | | 36 | | 48 | | 60 | | | Rat |

# Acknowledgements

First, I want to thank Karen Martin and Daniel Lenard for encouraging me to write this book and share the concepts. You were my earliest support, and helped me believe this dream was worth all the effort.

Second, I want to thank all my clients who gave me permission to share their stories, in hopes of helping other women. Your courage and commitment to personal growth are a constant inspiration to me. I learn *so* much from you! And I am so proud of all the work you do to build healthy relationships. You are all "sheroes" to me!

Thank you to my talented niece, Debbie Wadsworth Penor, for the Man-imal drawings. They are wonderful!

Thank you to my fabulous daughters, Kitty and Jillena, for all your support, your precious feedback, and for allowing me to share your stories. To quote from Seinfeld: "Your mother was right!"

Thank you to my wonderful son, Joseph, for being a great Gorilla. I'm so proud of the Ideal Man you are. You are a constant joy and proof that there are good men in every generation.

Thank you to Nick, for your computer genius in helping me with my website, The Quizzes, formatting this book, etc. I couldn't have done it without you!

Thank you to all the staff at The Difference Press, your guidance and support are amazing!

And finally, more than all the rest, thank you to my husband Dixon, my personal Ideal Man, business partner, co-coach, and Panther. You listened and gave me perspective, edited every word, encouraged me, and supported me in every way possible!

Your wisdom and heart can be found on every page throughout this book.

# About the Authors

Angeline Hart and Dixon Schwenk are a husband and wife team of almost 25 years. It is the second marriage for both, and between them, they have a lot of experience in the fields of personal growth and psychology.

From their own separate and shared history of relationships, they have developed highly effective methods for coaching. Both spent years in the dating scene, making mistakes and learning from them. They share with you the wisdom and skills they gained, which will help you avoid pitfalls and frustrations.

Within the writing team, Angeline provides a keen, no- nonsense writing style while Dixon tends to smooth the ruffled edges with a more lyrical view.

As a coach, Angeline is gifted with laser vision and unusual clarity in identifying the central issues within a challenging situation. She then gives support as she acknowledges each step forward in her client's work toward healthy resolution. It is almost a form of re-parenting, as Angeline shares the positive style of nurturing wisdom she received while growing up. Her clients feel her love and it allows them the space to create self-love and lasting change.

On the other hand, Dixon offers heartful insight to the struggles of clients who have previously been abused. Coming from a dysfunctional home, he is able to relate to the challenges of overcoming boundary invasion and long-term emotional abuse. When working with couples, Dixon also provides valuable balance as an advocate for the male perspective.

They live in San Diego, with their cat, Jasper.

61190578R00177

Made in the USA
Charleston, SC
16 September 2016